THE SECRETS OF
VESUVIUS

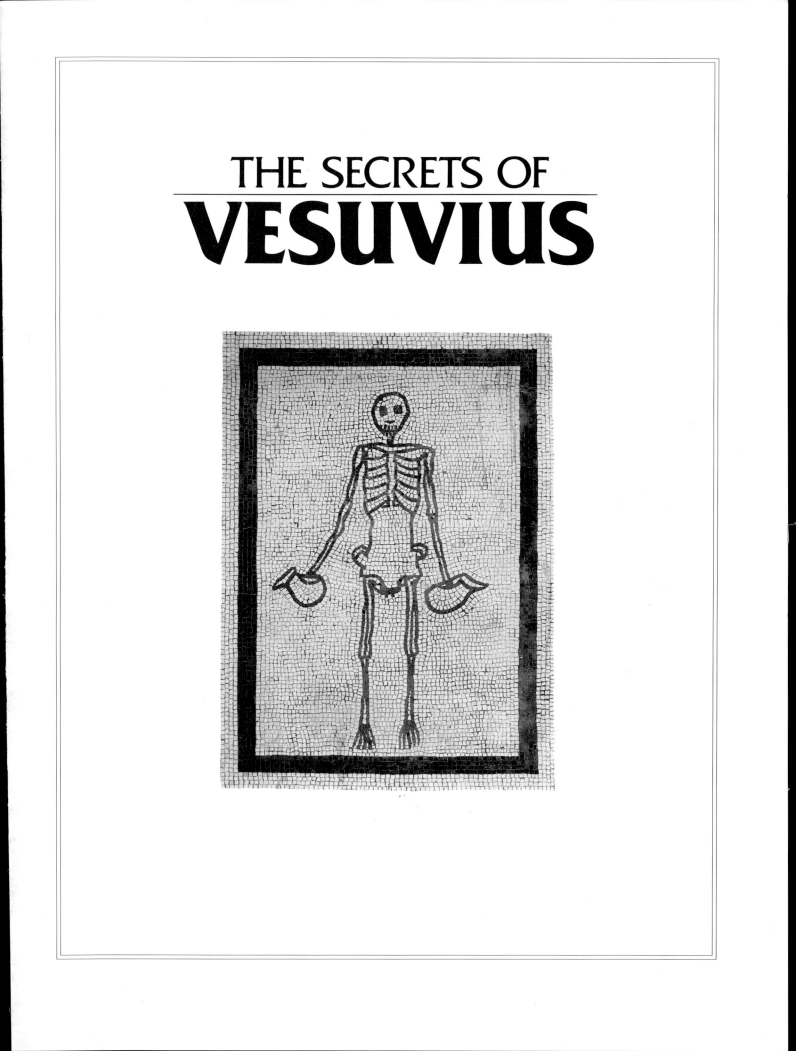

First published in Canada by
Random House of Canada Ltd.,
1265 Aerowood Drive, Mississauga, Ontario L4W 1B9

Canadian Cataloguing in Publication Data
  Bisel, Sara
    The secrets of Vesuvius

(A time quest book)
ISBN 0-394-22198-2

1. Vesuvius (Italy) — Eruption, 79 — Juvenile literature. 2. Pompeii (Ancient city) — Juvenile literature. 3. Italy — Antiquities — Juvenile literature. I. Title. II. Series: A time quest book (Mississauga, Ont.).

DG70.P7B58 1991   j937'.7   C90-094860-4

DESIGN AND ART DIRECTION: Gordon Sibley Design Inc.
ILLUSTRATION: Ken Marschall, Laurie McGaw, Jack McMaster, Margo Stahl
EDITORIAL: Hugh M. Brewster, Nan Froman
PRODUCTION: Susan Barrable, Donna Chong
TYPESETTING: On-line Graphics
PRINTER: Khai Wai Litho Pte. Ltd.

Endpapers: A mosaic with an actor's mask from Pompeii.
Previous page: This mosaic showing a skeleton with two wine jugs was found in the Bay of Naples area.
Right: A painting of the eruption of Mount Vesuvius in 1779.
Inset: A detail of a Roman mosaic.
Pages 6, 7: A painting of the ancient town of Herculaneum.
Pages 8, 9: The ruins of Herculaneum today.
Page 9, top inset: A wall painting of two young people from Pompeii.
Page 9, bottom inset: An aerial view of the crater of Vesuvius.

Produced by
Madison Press Books
40 Madison Avenue
Toronto, Ontario
Canada M5R 2S1

Printed in Singapore

THE SECRETS OF
VESUVIUS

by Sara C. Bisel

with Jane Bisel and Shelley Tanaka

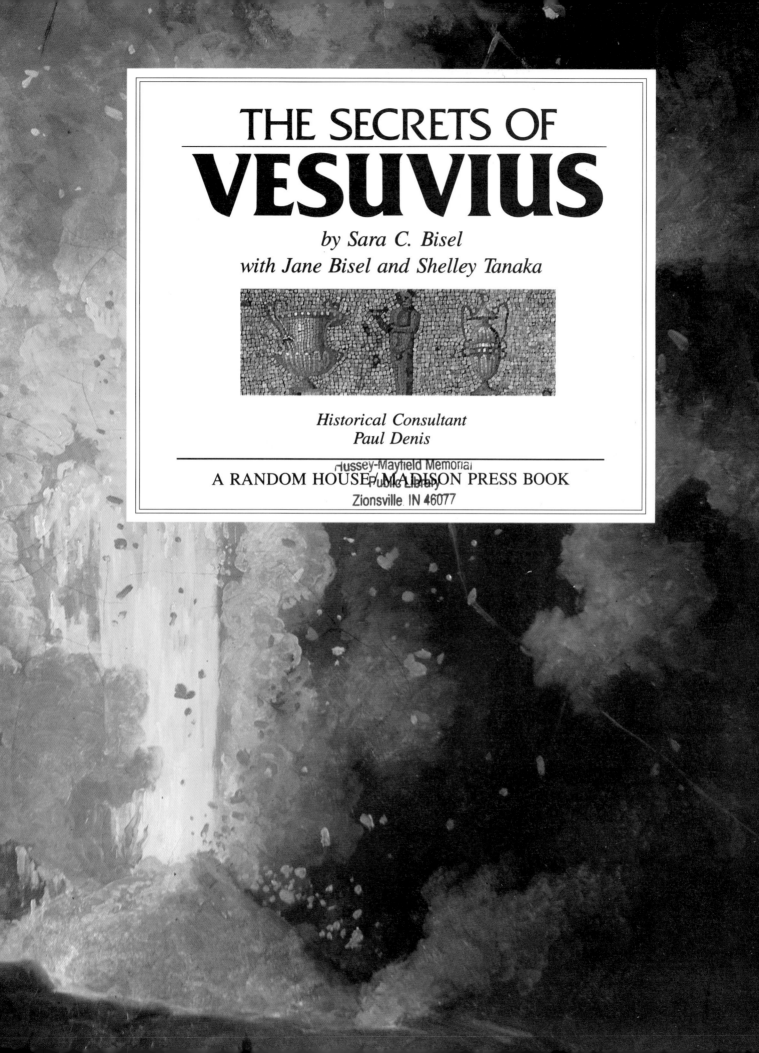

Historical Consultant
Paul Denis

A RANDOM HOUSE/MADISON PRESS BOOK

To the
Herculaneans of A.D. 79,
who still have stories
to tell . . .

Contents

In the seaside town of Herculaneum, this summer morning seemed like any other. On the beachfront the fishermen pulled up their boats in front of the seawall. Breezes from the bay cooled the wealthy Romans relaxing in the gardens of their elegant summer villas. No one suspected that within hours the top of nearby Mount Vesuvius would blow off, burying the town and many of its people under an enormous avalanche of scorching mud and ash.

oday the town of Herculaneum sits silently under the cone of the volcano that killed it. On the walls of its ruined villas, ghostly paintings and mosaics remind us of the thousands of people who once lived here. But what were these ancient Herculaneans really like and what happened to them on that fateful day in August, A.D. 79? Did most of them escape? One day an astonishing new discovery brought anthropologist Sara Bisel face to face with the actual victims of the fiery rage of Vesuvius.

CHAPTER ONE

• • • • • • • • • • •

A New Assignment

Athens, Greece, June 1982

The telegram lying at my door was marked "Urgent." As I bent down to pick it up, I hoped that it wasn't bad news. After spending a long hot day on my knees in the dusty ruins of an ancient Greek town, I was in no mood for surprises. When I ripped open the envelope I saw that it was from the National Geographic Society in Washington, D.C. They wanted me to telephone them immediately about a special project.

My job is to excavate and study the bones of people who lived and died many centuries ago.

Human bones are my speciality. In fact, I'm often called "the bone lady" because most of my work involves examining and reconstructing old skeletons. Believe it or not, bones are fascinating. They can tell you a great deal about someone, even if the person has been dead for thousands of years.

I can examine a skeleton and find out whether a person was male or female. If she was female, for example, I can tell you

Why are they in such a hurry, I asked myself. As an archaeologist and anthropologist I have been involved in many expeditions. But my jobs are almost never emergencies. If something has been lying in the ground for a few thousand years, another week or two usually doesn't make much difference.

As I shut the door to my tiny apartment, I calculated the time difference between Athens, Greece, and Washington, D.C., and then dialed the long-distance number. My contact at the National Geographic Society wondered if I could spare a few days to examine some human skeletons that had just been found at the town of Herculaneum in Italy. Skeletons in Herculaneum, I thought to myself. Now *that* would be interesting!

about how old she was when she died, whether she had children, what kind of work she might have done and what kind of food she ate. I can even glue dozens of small pieces of a skull back together like a jigsaw puzzle and show you what that person looked like.

The editor at *National Geographic* explained that workmen digging a drainage ditch near the ruins of Herculaneum had accidentally discovered some skeletons lying on what had once been the town's beachfront. Nearby, archaeologists had later uncovered some boat storage chambers in the ancient seawall. Much to their surprise, there were more skeletons inside these cave-like rooms. Here people had found shelter from the terrifying eruption of Mount Vesuvius in A.D. 79. As they lay

I point out the different parts of a human skull to a group of young anthropology students.

huddled together in the dark, they were smothered by an enormous surge of scorching gas and ash from the volcano. Flowing hot ash, rock and pumice then buried them. Today, almost two thousand years later, the tangled remains of these ancient Romans lie as they fell, preserved in the wet volcanic earth.

This was an amazing discovery. Although archaeologists have been digging out Herculaneum for centuries, very few bodies had ever been found. As a result, experts had decided that almost all of the Herculaneans must have escaped before the disaster. We now knew that this was not true.

But even more exciting for me was the chance to study the actual skeletons of real ancient Romans. Because the Romans cremated their dead, they left behind plenty of urns full of human ashes but very few complete remains. So these Herculaneans represented the first large group of Roman skeletons ever found.

"I'll book a seat on the next flight to Naples," I said to the *National Geographic* editor and then slammed the receiver down. I quickly rolled up a few T-shirts and several pairs of jeans and stuffed them into my bag. I knew that I had to leave for Italy right away. Now that the skeletons had been

exposed to the air, they had to be properly preserved as soon as possible or they would quickly disintegrate and turn to dust. If that was allowed to happen, a priceless opportunity to find out exactly what the ancient Romans had looked like and how they had lived would be lost.

It was strange, I thought grimly, that Vesuvius, the volcano that had caused one of the biggest natural disasters in the world, was now giving me

The town of Herculaneum is named after the legendary strongman Hercules. This vase shows Hercules strangling a lion.

the most exciting assignment any physical anthropologist could ever dream of. I would be the first person to recreate the lives of these men, women and children who had lived and died so long ago. I knew that bones could talk. If I listened carefully, they would whisper their secrets.

What would these skeletons tell me?

CHAPTER TWO

· · · · · · · · · · · ·

"There is a fire under your houses"

Herculaneum, August 23, A.D. 79

Petronia pushed her way through the morning crowds, trying not to drop the heavy load of stuffed dates that she had just picked up from the grocer. They had been specially prepared for a party her mistress was giving. Even though the banquet wasn't to take place for two days, the whole household had been in an uproar all week.

The kitchen slaves had been furiously preparing the exotic menu, and it seemed as though her mistress had summoned every musician and dancer between Naples and Pompeii in the search for the perfect after-dinner entertainment. She had been fussing over her wardrobe for days, and had even ordered an expensive new necklace to be made by

Alessandro, the town's finest gem-cutter.

Petronia stumbled over a paving stone. She was used to carrying heavy loads, but the basket was too full, and the glistening dates kept threatening to topple onto the street. She knew that the cook would probably count each one, and that it would mean another beating if any were missing.

Blowing a strand of hair out of her eyes, Petronia stopped and put the basket down. Leaning against a doorway, she held her hair off her perspiring neck.

All around her, the streets of Herculaneum were busy. Many tourists had come down from Rome and Naples for the Festival of the Divine Augustus. Even though the popular Emperor Augustus had died long ago, the entire Empire celebrated his memory every year. All week there had been special sports events in the *palaestra* and pantomimes in the theater, to say nothing of endless feasting and drinking.

A stray dog came sniffing around Petronia's tunic, and she kicked it away with the side of her foot. As she leaned back again, the paving stones beneath her seemed to rumble and groan, and she could have sworn that the doorway she was leaning on trembled slightly.

Petronia stood upright and looked around her. Had anyone else felt it?

But the crowds were going about their business as usual. Shoppers shoved each other aside on the street, while a group had gathered around a man playing a flute. Beside him a sickly-looking child with a wrinkled, old man's face half-heartedly beat a tambourine. From a wooden cart, an old peasant farmer was selling the first grapes of the season, picked from the vineyards on nearby Mount Vesuvius.

Petronia gingerly rubbed her jaw. A week ago she couldn't believe that any pain could be worse than her two rotting back teeth. She had tried every remedy she had heard of. She had plugged them with earthworm ash. She had even tried wrapping sparrow dung in a piece of wool and wearing it around her neck to ward off the pain. Finally, in agony, she had begged Cook to pull out the teeth for her.

And Cook had obliged — all too cheerfully, Petronia thought ruefully — cutting her gums so she could get a better grip with a nasty-looking instrument she had borrowed from a Greek slave who claimed to be a doctor.

Petronia sighed. Her mouth was still so sore that she hadn't been able to eat much all week. On top of that, the household had been so busy that she had scarcely slept in days....

Was she so tired and hungry that the buildings themselves seemed to move? But now she had better hurry home before the baby woke up. As she bent down to pick up her basket, she noticed that several dates had toppled off the pile onto the street. Hurriedly she picked them up, wiped them on her tunic and tucked them back in with the others.

Petronia buys a large basketful of stuffed dates from the grocer for her mistress's party.

"Tell your fortune, pretty one?" Hard, thin fingers gripped Petronia's shoulder, and a haggard face thrust itself in front of the young girl's. The woman's lips, clumsily painted with red ochre, curled back in a gummy, buck-toothed smile. Petronia recoiled at the stench of sour wine that hit her like a wave.

"I'm in a hurry," she muttered, trying to

Today Herculaneum lies silent *(above)*, but a Roman mosaic *(left)* calls to mind the musicians who once played in the streets of the ancient town.

wrench herself out of the woman's powerful grip. Festivals always seemed to bring even more lunatics to town than usual.

"Come on, girl. No charge for a sweet young thing like yourself. Let old Portia look into your future. I could teach you many things, if you let me. Ah, there is nothing like youth," she sighed, running her gnarled fingers through Petronia's dark hair.

"Let me go!" shouted Petronia. "Look, I told you —" And the fierce hold on her shoulder was

suddenly broken as a hairy, muscular arm came between the two women.

"Move on, you worm-eaten hag," said a rough male voice. "Can't you see this girl has better things to do than talk with the likes of you?" A hawk-faced man stared down at the two of them. His heavy iron sword looked deadly even in the scabbard that hung from his belt.

The old woman's watery eyes glinted madly. "You'll be sorry!" she shrieked. "The gods punish those who turn their backs on fate! Our wellsprings are running dry. The sea is boiling. There is a fire under your houses. I have listened to the heart of the mountain, and it beats in rage! Haven't you felt —" Her words were torn from her in a spasm of coughing. A couple of bystanders laughed, and a man poked the woman viciously with his staff as she turned suddenly and disappeared into the crowd.

Petronia cast a grateful look at the soldier, who simply narrowed his eyes and gave her a gap-toothed grin before heading into a nearby tavern. As he bent his head to walk under the awning, she noticed that he dragged his left leg just slightly.

Though the sea breezes were cool, Petronia's skin felt hot and prickly. Settling her basket on her hip and clutching it tightly, she quickened her step.

"Where in Isis' name have you been, girl?" cried the cook, as Petronia heaved her basket onto a table that

Petronia's mistress might have resembled the wealthy Roman woman shown playing a stringed instrument in this wall painting. Her young daughter stands behind her.

"You're in trouble again, Petronia," whispered Ia, one of the older kitchen slaves. "The baby has been awake for ages, screaming his head off. The chickens have broken out of their pen, and the master's horses have been rearing in their stalls all morning. What took you so long?"

"You try lugging that basket through a street full of beggars and madwomen," Petronia retorted. She grabbed a handful of grapes off the table while the cook's back was turned, as Ia stared in disbelief and horror.

"She was taking in a juggling show, I'll bet," snickered Lena, another slave who was sitting on a stool plucking chickens. "But she'll pay for it now. The mistress will wipe that pretty smile off your face with the back of her hand."

As if on cue, a shrill shout came from the garden.

"Is Petronia back yet? Where is that lazy girl?!" Petronia straightened her shoulders and went to answer her mistress's summons.

In the garden, Lavinia Claudia was furiously dandling the whimpering baby Julius on her knee. At the sight of the slave girl, she stood up. Then she gave Petronia a sharp cuff on the side of her head, scratching the girl's ear with the edge of one of her rings. Petronia stared silently at the ground. She knew better than to invite more rage by trying

was already laden with baskets of eggs, and piles of garlic and onions.

Two dates rolled out of the basket onto the floor, where they were greedily gobbled up by Ferox, the guard dog. The cook's eyes glinted angrily, but Petronia simply turned away and absently patted the dog's ears.

to apologize or make excuses for herself.

"Lena tells me you have been amusing your-self in town, leaving the others to do your work for you."

Petronia raised her head in disbelief.

"If it happens again, you will have to be taught a lesson. A severe one." She thrust the baby at Petronia. "Here, take him. The wet nurse has fed him, and he needs to be changed. Be quick about it, because I need you to do an errand. Two guests have already sent word that they are going back to Rome before the party. I think they're cowards, full of crazy talk about ground tremors and other stupid nonsense. Even my husband wants to return to Rome before the week is out. But I have spent far too much time and money on this party to cancel it now. So we will have to have the banquet tomorrow."

In the garden of a once lavish home in Herculaneum, weeds grow in a fountain where water used to play.

Petronia groaned to herself. Wait until Cook heard this news. There would be no sleep for any of them now.

"Word has been sent to most of the guests already, but Flavia Theodora is not at home. I want you to take a message to her to tell her about the change in plans. She will be at the theater this afternoon." And with that, Lavinia Claudia turned on her heel and swept out of the garden toward the kitchen to break the news to the cook.

Petronia sat down on the edge of the marble fountain. The garden suddenly seemed very still and peaceful with her mistress's departure. A goldfish glistened in the pool as it caught the reflection of the sun. The scent of oregano and thyme growing in the carefully tended beds, the pink and white flowers, the gentle trickle of the fountain at her back…

Perhaps, she thought wistfully, if she ever managed to drag her weary bones through this world, the land of the dead would look like this.

A tiny hiccup suddenly made her look down at the very wet bundle in her arms. Sighing, she gave little Julius a quick peck on the forehead.

"It's a bath for you, little baby," she crooned. "You smell."

Two hours later, Petronia made her way through town once again. The streets were less busy now. Most people were at the theater or the swimming pool or the baths, or simply seeking the coolest spot they could find for a few hours' rest.

As Petronia neared the theater, she could hear the laughter and shouts of the crowd, and her pulse quickened. She had never been inside the theater before, but she had heard plenty of gossip about the spectacles that took place there.

She stopped for a moment to marvel at the high rows of arches far above her. Then she headed toward one of the gates, drawn by a glimpse of enormous marble columns inside.

"Hold it, girl," shouted a guard at the door. "No slaves allowed. You know that."

"But I have a message for the lady Flavia Theodora," protested Petronia. "An urgent message from my mistress."

"A likely tale," laughed the guard. "Be off with you." He shoved Petronia roughly aside and turned back to his conversation with a fellow guard. "Not the crowd I would have expected today, given the festival. Half the seats are empty."

Petronia made a face at the guard behind his back and wheeled around, very nearly colliding with a tall figure wearing a dust-covered tunic and cloak. It was the hawk-faced soldier from the

AT THE THEATER

Herculaneum's theater (bottom) was elegantly decorated with marble and bronze statues. A rehearsal was probably in progress at the very moment that Vesuvius erupted. Today you can see the theater's buried ruins from underground tunnels.

The mosaic (left) shows actors getting ready for a performance. In the painting (above), the leading actor has just taken off his mask in the dressing room.

Dressing rooms

The *frons scaena* or backdrop was richly decorated.

The *cavea* or seating area

Stage

A *velarium* or awning kept the sun off the audience.

Sometimes actors performed in the orchestra.

The cutaway shows that you could walk around the theater through these galleries.

street, and once again he eyed her with a half-amused smile.

Bending her head, Petronia turned to get out of the man's way, but not before he leaned toward her and said in a low voice, "Try the stage door. Around the back."

By the time she realized he was talking to her and looked up, he had already disappeared through the theater entrance.

Petronia wandered around to the back of the theater. Sure enough, there was an unguarded entrance. Climbing a short flight of stairs, she could see the male actors frantically scrabbling around in a sea of masks, backdrops, hoists, cymbals, drums, wigs and robes. Resisting the temptation to explore backstage, where everyone seemed too busy to notice her, she slipped around the side of the stage into the open audience area.

It was even more magnificent than she had dreamed. Above her head, a huge awning, like the wing of a giant bird, stretched over the theater. Around the semicircular building, arches and pillars were decorated with intricate stucco work. Behind the raised stage stood marble and bronze statues and vases, each set in its own niche. The smooth white alabaster and black and purple marble shimmered in the sunlight that streamed through the gaps in the awning.

On the stage, the actors were performing the story of Daedalus and Icarus. It was a popular story, and Petronia knew it well. After offending the king, Daedalus and his son, Icarus, had been imprisoned. To escape, Daedalus made two pairs of wings out of feathers and wax. But when they tried to fly away, Icarus, in spite of his father's warning, flew too close to the sun. The wax in his wings melted, and he tumbled into the sea.

The crowd cheered now as Daedalus explained his escape plan to his son. At the back of the theater, Petronia spotted Flavia Theodora. She was

When they were on stage, Roman actors often wore masks like the one in this mosaic from Pompeii.

with her two young maids, Iris and Apollonia.

Petronia pushed by the vendors selling sweets and nuts, passed the front rows that were reserved for important officials, and climbed up the steps to the section that was set aside for women, children and ordinary citizens.

Flavia Theodora looked bored. Behind her stood Iris, who waved at Petronia with one hand while she held a green parasol over her mistress with the other.

Petronia explained that the banquet was now to be held the following evening.

"I, too, was planning to leave for Rome early tomorrow," said the woman, shaking her head dramatically. "There is talk of

Flavia Theodora's two slaves keep her cool as she watches the play from the very back of the theater, in the section reserved for women, children and ordinary citizens.

another earthquake. I suppose you're too young to remember the last one. We were in Rome at the time, but the damage to our house and statues was dreadful, to say nothing of the looting that occurred after…"

Flavia Theodora droned on. Behind her, Iris thrust out her lower jaw and opened and closed her mouth like a fish, mocking her mistress.

"… but I hear that Lavinia has outdone herself with this dinner, so I will postpone my trip one more day. Tell your mistress I will attend. Providing, of course, that your master isn't planning to read any of that boring poetry of his as after-dinner entertainment. Now be off quickly. You're blocking my view." And with a wave of her ring-laden hand, she dismissed the slave girl.

Petronia hurried home through the nearly empty streets. As she walked past the Forum Baths, she could hear the slaps and groans of men having massages and exercising with weights, as well as the thumps and curses of what sounded like an ugly brawl.

Suddenly, Petronia had the eerie feeling that she was being watched. Looking back, she saw the crazy soothsayer, Portia. With a wineskin in her hand, the woman eyed Petronia shrewdly from the shadow of the doorway.

Her lips formed a thin smile, and then she winked at the young girl.

Petronia felt cold, and her jaw suddenly started to throb again. She knew there were such things as witches — old crones who could turn men into animals or cast spells with their evil eye.

Remembering the old woman's shrill cries of doom that morning, Petronia began to run.

CHAPTER THREE

"Strange things are happening"

Petronia awoke with a start. Someone was shaking her straw sleeping pallet, shaking her awake.

She sat up, but the room was quiet. Through the open door she could see a patch of sky above the garden. It was not yet dawn. The room was murky, and she could barely make out the sleeping forms of Ia and Lena beside her.

Petronia sighed and lay back down, her bones aching with weariness. Today was the big day. Once she got up there would be no rest until the banquet was over and all the guests had eaten and drunk enough to make themselves ill. Even then, the slaves would be busy cleaning the thrown scraps of food off the floor before the dog scattered them all over the house. It would be a long time before any of them slept again.

Petronia lay on her side and prodded the tender spot in her gums with her tongue. She stared at the wall of her sleeping alcove. As she did, she noticed a crack that hadn't been there before, snaking down the wall. Idly, she ran her finger along it, and bits of stone dust fell onto her arm.

"Get up, you lazy mules!" It was Cook at the door of their cubicle, her rough, red hands resting on her hips. Ia and Lena groaned awake and stumbled to the kitchen, while Petronia crept to the nursery to check on Julius before he woke the mistress and master.

By mid-morning the sun had risen in a clear, bright-blue sky. From the solarium, Petronia could see that the bay was as calm as glass. It was going to be hot. The cicadas were already singing in the cypress trees. In the distance behind her, Mount Vesuvius lay covered in silvery-green olive groves and vineyards.

Petronia went back to the kitchen to help carry

A ROMAN BANQUET

The Romans are famous for their lavish banquets which often lasted long into the night. Diners reclined on couches around a low table while slaves brought them delicious food and drink. After dinner, dancers, musicians or poets entertained the guests.

The walls of the dining room in this Herculanean home are richly decorated with mosaics.

the food into the dining room. On long tables lay platters of snails and oysters, ham from Gaul, pomegranates from Libya, roast parrot, flamingos boiled with dates, roast wild boar bathed in a sauce of wine, raisins and mint. On one side table sat enormous fruit trays with melons cunningly carved to resemble birds and placed on nests of grape leaves and peacock feathers. On another table stood a row of wine-filled silver vessels decorated with skeletons, which guests would pass around at the end of the banquet to celebrate the good life in this world. After all, who knew what awaited them after death?

In the kitchen, Lena and Ia were cleaning more silver dishes.

"If you've nothing better to do, Petronia, you can take this broom and check the dining room for spiders," Cook ordered.

As Petronia walked past Lena to fetch the broom, her foot caught on something. Before she could recover her balance, she had upset a jug of olive oil that had been standing near the edge of the table.

Everyone stared, frozen, as the greenish-yellow liquid began to ooze onto the floor. Finally Cook leaped over and set the jug upright, but she didn't scold Petronia, and her eyes were wide with uncertainty.

"It's a bad omen," murmured Ia, and even Lena looked frightened.

"I've heard the talk in town," Cook said. "Strange things are happening. There have been earth tremors. This morning I went to the well and there was no water. Two slaves working in the master's olive groves have...disappeared."

"Run away?" gasped Ia.

Left: At a Roman banquet young slaves serve wealthy guests who would have dined from silver dishes such as these *(above)* and used glass drinking cups like the one shown *(below)*.

Cook nodded, and the three slave girls were silent. They knew what happened to runaway slaves, especially the strong men who were valuable items on the slave market. They would be hunted down and caught. Petronia had seen captured runaways being flogged and tortured, their foreheads branded so that everyone would know that they were criminals.

"Petronia!" screeched the mistress's voice from the garden. The girls were startled out of their thoughts. Lena and Ia went back to work, while Cook wiped up the spilled oil.

In the garden, the mistress looked frazzled and cross.

"I want you to go to the gem-cutter's to fetch my necklace," she ordered. "Care for it with your life, because it cost plenty. Far more than those cheap rings that Flavia Theodora keeps flashing in my face," she noted smugly. "But be quick. There is still plenty to do here before the guests arrive."

Petronia's face brightened. What luck! She loved going to the gem-cutter's.

It meant she would see Tiro.

The gem-cutter's shop was quiet as Petronia walked through the doorway. By the wall dozens of precious stones were displayed on a large marble table; in the corner stood a bronze candelabrum that was even finer than anything her master possessed.

"Is anyone here?" she called out softly.

This carved marble relief shows a slave carrying a heavy load of dates into a shop. The shopkeeper will measure the dates in a *modius*, the Roman measure sitting on a tripod on the floor. He will then sell the dates in small containers.

"Petronia, is that you?" A small voice came from a tiny room that opened off the main shop.

Peering in, Petronia saw the gem-cutter's son, Tiro, lying on his elegant wooden bed. He had been sickly ever since she had known him, but since spring he had grown steadily weaker, and now he rarely got up. She knew he was her age, but his frailness made him seem much younger. Today his skinny limbs were covered by a thin sheet, and his blond hair lay lank and damp on the pillow. She thought his pale skin looked even more waxen than usual.

"Of course it's me," she replied, forcing a smile to her face. "Look, I've brought you a present." And from the folds of her tunic she produced two stuffed dates that she had carefully stolen behind the cook's back before leaving the house.

Tiro's smile was wan and he didn't even lift his head from the pillow. Beside him on a small table was a bowl of chicken soup, untouched.

"Thank you, Petronia, but I'm not very hungry. Perhaps Grandmother would like them."

The old woman sat nearby on a wooden stool. She was weaving at a small loom.

Petronia held the dates out to the woman, but she just shook her head silently and went on working.

"Tiro, you have to eat something," Petronia begged. "Would you like me to feed you some of this soup?"

"Petronia, how good to see you!"

Petronia encourages her friend, Tiro, to eat some soup.

Alessandro, Tiro's father, stepped briskly into the room. "I see you've been visiting my boy. Doesn't he look well? He gets stronger every day. I expect to have him back helping me in the shop before long."

Tiro turned his face to the wall. His grand-mother's nimble fingers slowed just slightly. The silence in the room was thick, and Petronia rushed to fill it.

"Yes, he does look much better. But I've come for —"

Alessandro's gaze clouded for a moment. Then he smiled. "Your mistress's necklace. A pretty fine piece of work, if I do say so myself. Let me get it for you."

She turned to follow the gem-cutter out of the room, but Tiro caught her hand. "Please, Petronia, can't you stay with me just for a while?"

"Of course I can," she soothed. She sat down on a stool and began to tell him all about the banquet preparations at the house. He listened peacefully, while she chattered on and tried not to think about what awaited her at home when she arrived back late.

It was almost noon by the time she left the shop, her heart pounding as she ran home.

Sick children died all the time, she reminded herself. It was the will of the gods. Tiro would be better off in the land of the dead than spending the rest of his life lying on that bed.

Still, the desperate brightness in his father's voice was hard to forget.

"I warned you, didn't I, you disobedient snake. You were supposed to return here immediately, not dawdle taking in the sights in town."

The mistress had barely glanced at the neck-lace before she turned on Petronia. "This time it will be a lesson you'll remember. There is a sud-den shortage of slaves in the master's olive press. After tonight, I am sending you to work over there.

Perhaps a few days of hauling olives will break that wicked spirit of yours."

Petronia swallowed a gasp. Only the strongest and toughest male slaves worked in the olive press. The work was back-breakingly hard. And to be the only woman…

Without being dismissed, she turned and went to the kitchen. She didn't want the mistress to see that she was trembling. Until now she had always been convinced that Lavinia could not do without her in the house. Petronia was the only one who was good with the baby, and they both knew it. But perhaps this time she had gone too far.

In the kitchen, Cook was feeling pleased with herself as she put the finishing touches on a few dishes. She even allowed the girls to break for a quick meal. Lena and Ia ate fruit and eggs and bread, while Petronia gingerly spooned thin porridge into the side of her mouth, trying not to chew on her tender gums. She couldn't remember the last time she had eaten a proper meal.

As the three slaves ate, they stared with glazed, exhausted eyes at the banquet's crowning delicacy — dozens of tiny dormice stuffed with minced pork, pine nuts and fish paste, which Cook was carefully arranging on a gold platter.

Then Ia and Lena prepared to take the mistress and master a light lunch, while Petronia went to fetch Julius from the wet nurse to put him down for his afternoon nap.

"Good luck with getting him to sleep," complained Hermia, the wet nurse, as she handed Petronia the baby. She adjusted her tunic hurriedly. "I'm glad I just have to feed him. He's been very fussy today."

Julius was stiff and wailing. Petronia carried him over to see his pet nightingale in the garden, but the bird just sat mournfully in his cage and refused to sing. In the nursery, she handed the baby a small dog rattle, usually the toy he liked best, but he flung it angrily across the room. She tried walking with him, singing to him, rocking him, but he would not settle.

"I know just how you feel, you wet monkey," she murmured softly at the red, runny-nosed face, as she rubbed his small rigid back. "I could cry myself, I'm so tired." Outside, Ferox was barking madly, and she could hear the master's horses whinnying in their stalls. The whole household is out of sorts today, she thought. From the garden, a peacock shrilled loudly.

"Sounds just like your mother," Petronia whispered to Julius.

Finally, when the baby's wails had died down to a whimper, Petronia gently put the small boy in his crib. He sighed, burped softly, and soon began to breathe quietly.

She tiptoed out of the room to head back to the kitchen. As she passed by the dining room, she could see that it was decorated with flowers. Extra cushions, couches and tables had been moved in for the banquet.

At that moment, the ground seemed to heave below her feet. Then the most deafening sound Petronia had ever heard shook the house. It seemed to

Above: The *atrium* in a Herculanean home. Rainwater came in through the opening in the roof and filled the pool below.

Right: Every Roman house had a shrine to the household gods.

Roman kitchens were small and cramped. Here slaves prepared delightful dishes with fruit *(above)* or fish and fowl *(below)*.

Above: This kitchen at Pompeii, with its metal pots still sitting on the stove, is similar to those found in Herculaneum.

come from the very bowels of the earth.

From the kitchen she could hear screams and the sound of shattering dishes. The mistress rushed into the dining room followed by two maids who had been doing her hair. She was wearing only her sleeveless undertunic. Strands of hair hung down from a half-secured bun, and a streak of red hair dye trickled down her cheek. Her eyes were wide with fear.

"In Juno's name, what is it? What is happening?" she cried.

The master emerged from the garden, his face a mask.

"We must go back to Rome," he announced. "I should have listened to the others at the baths. Many of them have left already. Gather everyone together. We will leave immediately. Slave, bring the horses!" he called, striding out of the room.

Lavinia's face was white and pinched. "Petronia, fetch all the valuables," she ordered. "Put everything here, on the table. The silver and gold, the statues of Isis, everything you can carry.

Cook, find some bags. Lena, get the baby, and… my jewel case. It's in my bedroom. Quickly!" she screamed.

Petronia began running around the house with the others, plucking statues from their stands, bronze lamps and dishes from the side table — anything valuable that wasn't too heavy to carry. Everything was brought to the dining room, where the mistress shoved as much as she could into large coarse sacks.

A second cracking sound shook the house, not as loud as the first, but longer. A strange stench filled the air, like rotten eggs. For the first time, Petronia noticed that the bright sunshine had disappeared, and the sky had turned an odd shade — not gray like storm clouds, or black like night, but dirty-brown, like …

Like death, she thought.

The master came into the room, staring at his wife and the piles of gold, bronze and marble valuables tumbling out of the sacks.

"By the son of Jupiter, are you crazy,

woman?" he roared. "Don't you understand what is happening? We have no time to save your baubles! The streets are already jammed with people. We must leave now!" And he began to lead the way out the back entrance.

"But the baby!" cried Petronia. "Lena hasn't come back! What about Julius?"

Lavinia's eyes were glassy and unfocussed. "Get him, Petronia. The others will go ahead. I'll wait for you."

Petronia ran to the nursery. The crib was empty. Panic filled her as she raced from room to room, but there was no one to be seen. Never before had the house seemed so huge, with so many rooms and alcoves. In her desperation she began to look in places she had already been, in crazy places — under cushions, in cupboards, under beds.

She had to find Julius. In her heart, she knew he was still in the house. Finally, by the front door, she heard a whimper from the door-keeper's room beside the entrance.

Archaeologists found this small wooden crib, with a baby's bones still inside, in one of Herculaneum's villas.

On the floor was Julius, lying on his back. Lena was nowhere to be seen. The baby gurgled and raised his arms when he saw her. As Petronia snatched him up, she noticed the mistress's open jewel case on the floor near his feet.

It was empty.

Petronia raced back to the dining room through the garden. As she ran past the fountain, she glimpsed the nightingale in the corner of the courtyard. The brown bird lay still on the floor of the cage.

By the dim light of an oil lamp, she could see that the dining room, like the rest of the house, had been abandoned. Calling for the mistress, for Cook, for anybody, she ran out the back entrance into the street.

Outside it was very dark, and the air was thick with a strange, hot dust that stuck in her throat and made her eyes water. Screaming, pushing crowds on donkeys, horses, even oxen and cows filled the streets. They were all heading inland for the edge of town and the road to Naples. Her mistress and master were nowhere to be seen.

As she was shoved along with the surging crowd, Petronia heard a strangled bark near the front door of the house. It was Ferox, furiously trying to twist around to bite at his leash. There were raw, bare patches on his coat where he had gnawed at his own fur in his frenzy.

Bending down, the girl untied his leash, and the dog soon disappeared howling into the crowd.

Petronia stood up and shifted Julius to her other hip. As she did so, she glanced back through a gap in the buildings toward Mount Vesuvius. What she saw made her heart almost stop with fear.

In the distance, the peak seemed disfigured, as if a giant axe had cleft the summit and ripped open the mountain's jaws. The mouth of the mountain was outlined in a blaze of red flame, and glowing rocks bubbled out below a gigantic plume of smoke and ash.

The earth gods had gone mad. There was only one thing to do. She was going to get as far away from the mountain as she could. Clutching Julius so tightly that he began to cry, Petronia turned away from the crowds and began to run toward the sea.

Right: With the townspeople fleeing around her, Petronia rescues Ferox, the guard dog.

CHAPTER FOUR

• • • • • • • • • • • •

The Rage of Vesuvius

Naples, Italy, June, 1982

. . .darkness fell, not the dark of a moonless or cloudy night, but as if the lamp had been put out in a closed room. You could hear the shrieks of women, the wailing of infants, and the shouting of men; some were calling their parents, others their children or their wives, trying to recognize them by their voices. People bewailed their own fate or that of their relatives, and there were some who prayed for death in their terror of dying. Many sought the aid of the gods, but still more imagined there were no gods left, and that the universe was plunged into eternal darkness for evermore.

Pliny the Younger
1st century A.D.

I put down my fork and reread the words that described a group of people trying to escape from the fury of Vesuvius on that August day so many years ago. A chill crept up my neck. I was no longer hungry.

I had been hoping to start examining the new skeletons soon after I arrived. But it was late by the time I checked into my hotel, and I knew that not much could be done until morning. You need good light for excavation work. So I'd had a bath, tucked a

I catch up on my reading in my small hotel room a few miles from the excavation site at Herculaneum.

few books under my arm and gone down to the hotel restaurant where I ordered a plate of pasta. Then I settled down for a crash review lesson on ancient Herculaneum and how the sudden eruption of Vesuvius had changed its fate forever.

The descriptions I was reading had been written by Pliny, a seventeen-year-old student who lived in Misenum, across the Bay of Naples. His uncle had sailed across the bay toward Herculaneum to try to help stranded friends, until his ship was cut off by "bits of pumice and blackened stones, charred and cracked by the flames." Did Pliny's uncle have any idea what he was sailing into, I wondered. Or, when he saw from afar the mountain explode and a column of ash and smoke rise twelve miles (twenty kilometres) into the air, could he simply not believe his eyes until he had taken a closer look?

Pliny's uncle eventually landed at Stabiae, several miles south of Herculaneum. Though "great sheets of flame" were flashing out from the peak of Vesuvius, he actually had a bath and went to sleep. But the people with him sat up in terror all night, while the buildings shook as if they were being torn out of the ground. When the door

to the uncle's room became choked by a layer of cinder and ash, they woke him up and fled, tying pillows on their heads as protection against the pumice stones that rained around them.

But Vesuvius eventually caught up with Pliny's uncle. In spite of his calm bravery, he was suffocated by sulphur fumes while trying to get back to his ship.

Meanwhile, about twenty miles (thirty-two kilometres) across the bay at Misenum, Pliny observed the various stages of the eruption, beginning with the appearance of the mushroom-shaped cloud of ash, followed by falling ash, pumice and stones. He described earth shocks so violent it seemed as if the world was not only being shaken, but turned upside down.

I thought it was amazing that the eyewitness account he wrote had come down through the centuries. Only recently did modern scientists realize how accurate Pliny's description was, after they had studied many other volcanoes themselves. I put down my book. From the window I could see

Mount Vesuvius, quiet now, looking more like a gentle slumbering hill than a deadly and still-active volcano.

Pliny's description of panicking crowds had been written about the people at Misenum, who had had to shake the ashes off their bodies so they would not be buried alive.

How much worse must it have been for the Herculaneans, who lived closer to the inferno, hemmed in between the mountain and the sea? Vesuvius's blast was so powerful that ash fell as far away as Africa and Syria.

I know many people who get shivers up their spines at the sight of a big lightning storm, or ten-foot waves crashing onto the seashore. But to have the very earth beneath you suddenly gush ash and fire, to have a glowing avalanche of ash and pumice, hotter than an oven, rip over the land at the speed of a galloping horse. . . .

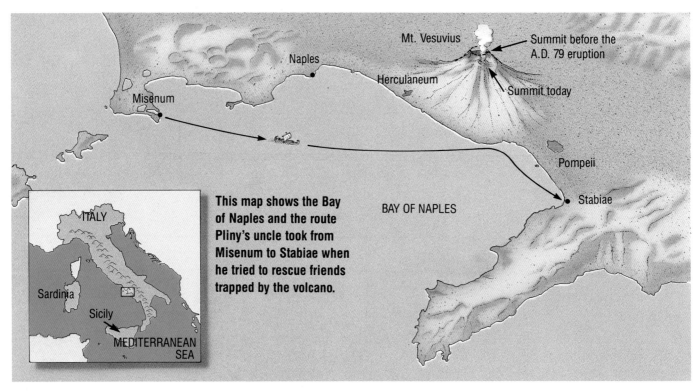

Mt. Vesuvius
Summit before the A.D. 79 eruption
Naples
Herculaneum
Summit today
Misenum
Pompeii
Stabiae
BAY OF NAPLES

This map shows the Bay of Naples and the route Pliny's uncle took from Misenum to Stabiae when he tried to rescue friends trapped by the volcano.

ITALY
Sardinia
Sicily
MEDITERRANEAN SEA

WHY DID VESUVIUS ERUPT?

Far below the earth's surface, gigantic plates of the earth's crust are constantly moving. Where these plates meet, one piece may rub against another, causing an earthquake. But if one plate pushes itself under another, it will melt and become liquid rock or magma. The super-hot liquid rock creates gas and steam, building pressure until it blasts through weak places in the earth's surface. These weak spots are the world's volcanoes.

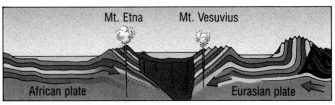

Mt. Etna   Mt. Vesuvius

African plate   Eurasian plate

Above: Vesuvius is located in an area of the world where two plates of the earth's crust meet.

When Vesuvius erupted, ash and gas came spewing out of the summit, forced straight up into the air by the pressure and heat of the blast. Eventually, this cloud cooled, and some of it collapsed, sending ash and hot gas racing down the slopes at speeds of up to seventy miles (110 kilometres) per hour, ripping the roofs off houses and overturning ships in the bay. These surges were followed by thick and glowing avalanches of fiery ash, rock and pumice — hot magma that has cooled so quickly that it is still full of volcanic gases, like a hard foamy sponge.

Vesuvius had not actually erupted for hundreds of years before A.D. 79, and the people of the area believed the volcano was extinct. But they could remember an earthquake seventeen years earlier that had caused much damage to the town. And in the days before the volcano erupted,

occasional rumblings and ground tremors were felt, creating the odd crack in a wall, or causing a statue to tumble off its stand. And other strange things happened: wells and springs mysteriously dried up, flocks of birds flew away, and animals were exceptionally restless.

We know now that the dry wells were caused by the increasing heat and pressure that were building deep in the earth, and that animals are always more sensitive than humans to changes in the earth and the atmosphere. But, I wondered, were the people in Herculaneum aware that something was about to happen? Before the mountain actually erupted, did it occur to anyone that it might be a good idea to leave town? How many waited until the streets were so crowded that escape was almost impossible? Were they spooked by the tremors, their suddenly dry wells, or the nervous actions of their animals? Did they think the gods were showing their anger?

We will probably never know exactly what the volcano's victims were thinking in those days before the eruption. We do know that the glowing avalanches that buried Herculaneum and the nearby city of Pompeii created two time capsules of ancient Roman life that have not changed in almost two thousand years.

Sealed by volcanic ash and rock, the buried buildings have been protected from the wind and rain that would have worn down the columns and statues over the centuries. Wooden doors, shutters, stairs, cupboards and tables have not been exposed to the air to rot away, or been destroyed by fire. And unlike other ancient towns, the roads and buildings have not been repaired, or torn down and replaced by something more modern.

Instead, Herculaneum and Pompeii look the way they did so many years ago. The roofs of the houses may be gone, the mosaic floors cracked and the wall paintings faded. But we can still walk down the streets over the same stones that the ancient Romans walked on. We can see a 2,000-year-old loaf of bread, now turned to stone, or eggs still in their shells waiting to be served for lunch.

Although both Herculaneum and Pompeii were buried by the volcano, their fates were quite different. Pompeii, a town of twenty thousand people, lay five miles (eight kilometres) away from the volcano, but the wind was blowing in its direction when the eruption occurred. Throughout the afternoon and evening of August 24th, ash and pumice rained down on Pompeii. This frightened many people, and some of them fled immediately. But it was not until early the next morning that the first flow of hot gas and ash overwhelmed the town, killing the two thousand people who had failed to escape.

The fallen bodies of the Pompeiians were buried under twelve feet (four metres) of ash and pumice. When the dead bodies rotted away, they left hollow places in the hardened volcanic rock. Archaeologists discovered these cavities in the 1860s and decided to pour in plaster to create

Mount St. Helens erupted in the United States in 1980, sending this mushroom-shaped cloud of ash into the sky. The people of Herculaneum would have seen the same kind of cloud coming from Mount Vesuvius.

lifelike models of the volcano's victims as they lay or crouched in the positions in which they died. Some appear to be gasping or choking in their final moments as they were suffocated by ash so hot that it singed their hair and burned the insides of their mouths. But the plaster also covered up what remained of the skeletons, preventing them from being studied by modern scientists.

Herculaneum, which was less than three miles (five kilometres) from Vesuvius, was upwind of the volcano. Most of the falling ash blew in the opposite direction, leaving less than an inch lying over the town by the end of the day. Instead, at about 1:15 early the next morning, a violent surge of ash

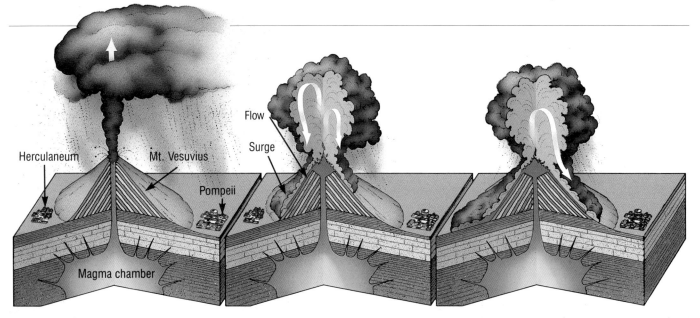

1. At midday on August 24, A.D. 79, Vesuvius erupts, sending a cloud of ash and pumice 12 miles (20 kilometres) into the air.

2. After midnight, the cloud collapses, sending a surge of ash and hot gas down the mountain, killing the Herculaneans. A flow of hot ash, rock and pumice eventually buries the town.

3. Early the next morning another surge kills the people of Pompeii. It, too, is followed by a flow of hot debris from the volcano.

and hot gas poured over the town. By the time the waves of hot mud followed, everyone was dead. In a few hours, Herculaneum was completely buried under sixty-five feet (twenty metres) of hot volcanic matter, which, when it cooled, covered the town like a cement shield.

And so the town lay tightly sealed, for about 1,500 years.

Then in 1709, a well-digger accidentally struck fine polished marble beneath the ground. An Austrian prince who was building a villa in the area realized that the marble was likely just the beginning of a major buried treasure, and he started to dig into the site.

Luckily for the prince, and unhappily for modern archaeologists and historians, the well-digger had found Herculaneum's ancient theater, one of the most luxurious and treasure-filled buildings in the town. The prince wanted art and fine building materials for

In the eighteenth century, these striking bronze statues of athletes were dug out from a lavish villa called the Villa of the Papyri.

his villa, so he hired diggers who bored tunnels through the theater, not knowing what it was, and not caring in the least about the damage they were doing to the structure itself.

The prince plundered the building of its bronze and stone statues and vases. Marble was ripped off the walls and pillars, and the treasures were carted off to the prince's own house or those of his rich friends. Before long these valuable artifacts were scattered in museums and private collections all over Europe.

The prince's raiders, burrowing through the site like greedy moles sniffing out treasure, did more damage to Herculaneum than the volcano itself.

More raiding expeditions followed, and it was only in 1860 that serious archaeological work began. But even with many of the most precious objects gone, the excavated town itself told historians a great deal about the ancient Romans and how they lived. Because the ruin had been snugly covered by a wet and heavy layer of earth, Herculaneum was even better preserved than Pompeii (which had suffered more damage under its airy blanket of ash and pumice).

Then just a few years ago came the most amazing discovery of all, when ditch-diggers accidentally found the group of skeletons on the ancient beachfront.

By the time these beach skeletons were found, scientists had discovered that we could learn a great deal about people by examining their bones.

We could do much more than make plaster casts. Now we can analyze the bones themselves and reconstruct the skulls to see what the people looked like.

This is where I came in. In the morning, I would help to dig up these bones and begin to study them. For the first time, we would know more about the Romans than what books and paintings and sculptures had shown us. We would be able to see the people themselves.

I would be one of the first modern people to look an ancient Roman in the face.

Archaeologists made lifelike models at Pompeii *(above and right)* by pouring plaster into the hollow shells of hardened volcanic rock that sealed Vesuvius's victims.

Possibly the dog *(right)* was a guard dog like the one shown in this Roman mosaic *(left)* which bears the Latin words *"cave canem"* or "beware of the dog."

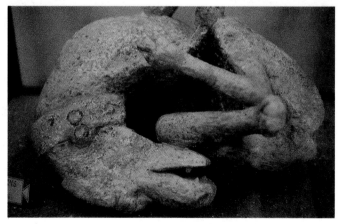

· · · · · · · · · · · · ·

CHAPTER FIVE

Exploring the Ghostly Town

Herculaneum, June, 1982

After breakfast the next day, I squeezed onto a Naples bus loaded with morning shoppers and headed for Herculaneum. It was time to get to work.

The excavation site doesn't look like much from a distance. It lies about sixty-five feet (twenty metres) below modern-day Ercolano, a crowded Naples suburb filled with peeling apartment houses overlooking the ruins. Much of the ancient town is still buried under these houses, and some of the people who live on top of the site are not pleased at the thought of losing their homes so that some archaeologists can dig for 2,000-year-old buildings and dirty skeletons.

Even surrounded by the fumes and honking of rush-hour traffic, and the laundry hanging from the apartment windows, I could still see why Pliny had described this place as "one of the loveliest regions of the earth." Vesuvius is so close that the town almost seems to be lying in her lap. The salt breezes still blow in from the Bay of Naples,

A friend and I pause to rest on an ancient fountain in what was once Herculaneum's bustling main street.

though the bay itself is now polluted.

When I got to the site, Dr. Maggi, the director of the excavation, was nowhere to be seen. Workmen sat around in small groups, drinking coffee out of thermoses. They eyed me curiously, then went back to their chat. I took a deep breath and decided to be patient. Later I would discover that waiting for Dr. Maggi's permission to begin work every morning was part of the routine. He made sure that excavation at the site was always closely supervised.

He arrived a few minutes later and introduced me to Ciro Formuola, the foreman of the work crew that was going to help me dig out the skeletons.

Herculaneum was covered by 65 feet (20 metres) of debris, while 12 feet (4 metres) of debris fell on Pompeii. Six different surges (the dark bands of ash on the diagram) poured down over Herculaneum, each followed by a scorching flow of debris. Only two of these surges reached Pompeii.

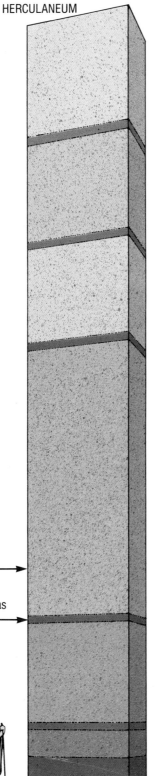

HERCULANEUM

Flow (hot ash, pumice and rock)

Surge (hot gas and ash)

POMPEII

These men were highly trained in doing delicate excavation work, and I knew I was lucky to have such experienced co-workers. In this business, a false move with a spade or trowel can do damage beyond repair.

I couldn't speak more than a few words of Italian, and none of the workmen spoke English. But we managed to communicate, mostly by smiling and hand-waving. Though later I discovered that a number of the local people were a little wary of a middle-aged American woman who kept human bones in her hotel room, the members of the crew were always helpful and patient with me, especially once they found out that I was willing to get my hands dirty with them.

"Shall we tour the site first, *dottoressa*, before going down to the beach?" Dr. Maggi asked.

I nodded. I knew that it was important for me to find out as much about the town as possible. If I was going to piece together the lives of the ancient Herculaneans, I had to know what kinds of work they might have done, where they might have lived and shopped, and how they could have spent their free time.

The ruins of Herculaneum and the Bay of Naples.

In A.D. 79, Herculaneum was a resort town of about five thousand people — mostly the rich, along with the slaves, artisans and shopkeepers who served them and provided their goods. There was no central market square, and only one set of steps led up from the beach, which meant it wasn't a trading or shipping town.

As Dr. Maggi and I walked down the gutter-lined streets, he pointed out the greengrocer, pastry shop, cloth merchant, clothes cleaner, blacksmith, stone cutter and tavern. I could easily picture the crowds that would have lined these streets every morning — shoppers, beggars, fortune tellers, street vendors and rich ladies being carried on litters by slaves. The fronts of the shops were open to the street. The Romans liked to spend as much time as they could outdoors, and often shopkeepers would wait for their customers out on the paving stones that lined the street.

We stopped at one of the many *thermopolia* — take-out restaurants where people could buy bread, dried fish, cheese, wine and hot food to take home. Eating take-out food was more of a necessity than a treat, though, since only wealthy homes had full kitchens. I could see a jar of walnuts still sitting on the counter, and a small peep hole in the wall behind, which would have been useful for keeping an eye out for shoplifters or listening in on a juicy bit of gossip. Another of these "snack bars" had holes in the marble counter where containers of hot wine would be set to keep warm.

Inside the *pistrinum*, or bakery, stood round millstones that were powered by slaves or blind-folded donkeys who walked in an endless circle to turn the stone and grind flour. This flour was used to bake breads, cakes, a kind of pizza (but without tomato sauce), and even dog biscuits! When the bakery was dug out, the bones of the donkeys were found still harnessed to the mills.

The tour of the main streets reminded me how little ordinary people have changed in two thousand years. Our lives today are not much different. We still have to shop, eat and earn a living. As I poked my head into each shop, I could almost hear the voices of the people who had worked there, complaining about unpaid bills, yelling at their children, shooing a stray dog out of the store. In the gem-cutter's shop, diggers had found a beautifully carved wooden bed in a small alcove off the front room. The skeleton of a teenage boy still lay on the bed. Beside him, a woman's skeleton had collapsed where she had been sitting on a stool in front of a small weaving loom. Nearby stood a small table with a bowl full of chicken bones.

Why hadn't these people tried to escape when Vesuvius erupted? Had the boy been too ill, the woman too old or frail to carry him? Had he been eating his lunch when the explosion occurred, perhaps being given a special treat of chicken soup to try to tempt his appetite?

Many of the poorer residents of Herculaneum lived in rooms behind or above their shops, or in larger buildings that had been divided into small apartments. These cramped, dark, low-ceilinged quarters were very different from the houses Dr. Maggi and I toured next — the homes of the rich.

I would love to have a house like one of these Roman villas. They were airy, beautifully laid out and comfortable, with lots of rooms.

There were dark, cool bedrooms with cozy sleeping alcoves, sun decks and terraces for lounging and taking in the view of the bay, dining rooms for entertaining, where diners would recline on couches while eating from low tables, formal rooms for receiving guests and showing off the

AN ANCIENT BAKERY

The Romans ground grain in large millstones to make flour for bread. Slaves or blindfolded donkeys turned these millstones *(right)*. The donkeys were blindfolded so that they would not be distracted. The baker then cooked the loaves inside a brick oven.

Below: This loaf of bread, which has survived from Pompeii, is now as hard as rock. Round loaves like this are still made in Italian bakeries.

Left: **In this painting, an official gives out free loaves of bread to win the people's support.**

most prized household statues, and small rooms especially designed to catch the sea breezes while you took your afternoon nap. The ancient Romans liked open spaces, and were sensible enough not to clutter their rooms with a lot of unnecessary furniture. Instead, the walls were painted with spectacular murals, and the floors were often decorated with intricate mosaics.

But the spots I liked best of all were the private gardens. These central courtyards, surrounded by fluted columns and sometimes enclosed by panes of glass, were as big as many modern backyards. Even now they look soothingly private and peaceful with their central fountains and goldfish pools. The courtyards were crisscrossed by gravel paths

lined with palm and cypress trees, as well as herbs, climbing vines and flowering plants. It must have been the height of luxury to sit out here, with a maid holding a parasol over your head to shade you from the brilliant sunlight, and with a servant bringing a tray of mulled wine, fresh fruit and cakes.

And many of these villas were just summer homes, I remembered — vacation cottages for people who had much grander dwellings back in the city.

As Dr. Maggi and I wandered from one room to the next, he pointed out some of the things that had been found in the houses — furniture and possessions that suggested the Herculaneans had left their homes in a great hurry. In some places it almost looked as if someone had just got up from lunch to answer a knock at the door or see to a crying baby, fully expecting to return in a few minutes.

In a dining room a table was set with spoons in preparation for lunch. In a kitchen, a kettle sat on a stove, just as it was left two thousand years ago. And in one house, archaeologists found a small wooden crib with a baby's bones still in it.

Who could have left a baby behind, I wondered.

But, while the shops and homes made me feel that the Romans must have been very much like us, it was Herculaneum's public buildings that made me realize how different Roman life was from ours.

Today, a town the size of Herculaneum will likely have a couple of schools, maybe a library, one main shopping street and probably an ugly strip of fast-food restaurants. But ancient Herculaneum boasted an elegant courthouse, a large theater, a magnificent sports complex complete with two swimming pools and a running track, two public bathhouses, as well as several streets lined with dozens of shops, restaurants and taverns.

In the elaborate public bathhouses, people of all ages, both rich and poor, would go regularly to get clean, play dice, lift weights, have a massage, play ball (using an inflated animal bladder), read, have a snack, exercise, or just gossip and visit. The baths had hot and cold running water (lead pipes carried water throughout the town), with separate rooms for hot, warm and cold baths. They also contained saunas, lockers and changing areas. Herculaneum had two baths — the Forum Baths in the

In 1750, from an underground tunnel near Herculaneum, Karl Weber drew plans of the majestic Villa of the Papyri. Millionaire J. Paul Getty built a museum in California based on these plans *(above)*.

Right: A wall painting showing a villa by the sea.

Right: When volcanic rock was chipped away from this room in the Suburban Baths, a beautiful statue of Apollo was discovered.

Volcanic flow burst through a window in the Suburban Baths throwing a heavy marble basin like this one *(above)* across the room. You can still see pieces of window glass in the bottom of the basin.

town itself, and the Suburban Baths on the beach, just outside the town walls. The Suburban Baths were exceptionally luxurious — more like an exclusive country club than a bath house — with a skylight and fountain, elaborate wall paintings, a swimming pool, marble basins, and a breathtaking view of the sea.

In the *palaestra*, a kind of public gym and athletic field, competitions would have been held during the mornings in the week just before Vesuvius erupted. Accompanied by trumpet music, athletes marched in to their various events — boxing, wrestling, racing and discus throwing. The playing field would have been filled with naked young men competing for olive-wreath crowns, while spectators watched from the shade of the surrounding portico. The *palaestra* also had a huge swimming pool in the shape of a cross. In the middle of the pool a bronze fountain shaped like a serpent sprayed water from five heads.

Archaeologists have found many ancient everyday objects in Herculaneum, including this small terracotta oil lamp.

After we had toured the town, Dr. Maggi showed me a storeroom where objects from the excavation site were being catalogued. Although the room was filled with beautiful glassware, gold coins and valuable jewels, it was the everyday objects that moved me the most — combs, mirrors, small oil lamps, dishes of beans and eggs, dice for a board game, buttons, ink pots (the Romans made ink out of soot, squid ink and wine dregs), fish hooks and broom bristles. These were things the Herculaneans wouldn't have bothered to save, even if they had had enough time.

My head was spinning by the time we finished our tour. "Well, Dr. Bisel." Dr. Maggi turned to me with a twinkle in his eye. He could tell I was eager to start work. "Perhaps you have seen enough. Shall we take a look at those boat shelters?"

As we walked down the steep slope to the ancient beachfront, which is 500 yards (460 metres) from the present shoreline, I could see the arched chambers where I knew so many skeletons lay waiting. In my excitement to reach them, I almost hurried past a makeshift wooden shed that jutted out from the wall. Inside, supported by a complicated arrangement of ropes and beams, a huge charred object lay on the ground like a beached whale, half buried in volcanic rock.

"What is that?" I asked Dr. Maggi.

He smiled proudly. "That is one of our greatest treasures. Not a human skeleton, but still very special."

It was a 2,000-year-old wooden boat that had been overturned and swept onto the beach during the volcano and then sealed by the avalanche. While it lay buried, the wood had carbonized, turning into fragile charcoal. It was now being studied by Richard Steffy, a specialist in ancient ships and boat construction.

Dr. Maggi introduced me to Richard, whose task was not very different from mine. My job was to preserve, reconstruct and study fragile skeletons. His was to study a vessel so fragile, it would crumble into thousands of pieces if anyone tried to lift it. He, too, had to be as careful and exact as a surgeon to find out as much as he could about the boat without damaging it. And, like me, Richard was a detective, putting together pieces of a puzzle that would eventually tell him what the boat was used for, and how it had got on the beach.

Richard led me around the sweeping blackened hull of the boat.

"It's probably a thirty-footer," he explained. "Large for a Roman boat, but very light. Half of it is still buried — we don't even know whether we've got the bow or the stern end here. And, of course, because we can't lift it, we can't see underneath. But the design is quite fancy, and the bronze nails are still in place."

"And if you could see inside it, what would you know?" I asked.

"Well, we would probably be able to tell how it was built and steered, what kind of sail it had, whether it was built for both sailing and rowing, whether it was a fishing boat or tug boat or wine carrier. We don't know much about small first-century Roman boats. This one could give us a lot of important information."

Richard told me that archaeologists have also found many timbers on Herculaneum's beach that might have been part of an ancient pier. He thought the town might even have been a place where ships were built.

"Could the Herculaneans have been trying to escape in this boat?" I asked.

But Richard didn't think so. After studying the layers of volcanic deposits, experts have decided that the boat was thrown onto the beach after the first glowing avalanche had buried everyone. Besides, the water would have been churned up by the eruption, making sea travel impossible.

It must have been awful, I thought. The people whose skeletons I was about to see must have run down to this beach in desperation, hoping against hope that they could get away.

And when they got here they discovered the horrible truth — that escape was impossible.

Below: Richard Steffy examines the fragile boat found on the beachfront. This wall painting from Pompeii *(inset)* shows what the boat from Herculaneum might have looked like under full sail.

CHAPTER SIX

• • • • • • • • • • • •

"The gods are punishing us!"

Herculaneum, August 24, A.D. 79

Petronia stumbled down the street toward the sea. The paving stones were slippery, covered with a thin layer of dust that made it hard for her to move quickly. The shouts and clatter of the crowds were now just a dull roar behind her. Beneath her bare feet, the earth seemed to be trembling, and in the distance she could hear a deep, crackling rumble. She knew it was the mountain, but she couldn't bear to look back.

In her arms, Julius began to bawl again.

"Shut up, please," she begged, covering his head with her arm to stifle his cries. The streets that she knew so well seemed unfamiliar, the darkened doorways on either side of her gaping like open mouths.

As she passed the entrance to the gem-cutter's shop, her steps slowed, almost against her will. The crowds had thinned. Only the odd person passed her blindly, caught up in flight.

She heard a faint cry coming from the shop. It was Tiro's voice. He was calling for his father.

Petronia stopped. She buried her face in Julius's warm, damp neck, begging her ears not to hear the cries. The baby suddenly felt like the heaviest burden she had ever carried.

"I can't..." she whispered softly. Her cheeks were wet.

Behind her, the mountain roared again. A nearby pillar cracked suddenly and toppled to the ground.

Petronia took one last look at the doorway to the shop. Clutching Julius to her more fiercely, she hurried past the entrance. Her heart lay cold in her chest, like a shard of ice.

She ran.

Then, ahead of her, Petronia saw a lone, slightly loping figure. The coarse tunic, the sword, the leather bag flung over the shoulder...

It was the hawk-faced man, the soldier. He, too, was heading toward the beach.

"Wait! Wait for us!" she called, running to catch up to him.

He turned and saw her and the baby. Without a word, he took her arm and pulled her along with him. Even with his bad leg, he could move much faster than she could.

As they scrambled down the steps to the beach, they could hear shouts. At the foot of the stairs was a large crowd of people who had run from the mountain and had now gone as far as they could. There were slaves, children, fishermen, people clutching coin boxes and other valuables. A young woman, barely older than Petronia herself, stood staring at nothing, her arms folded over her pregnant belly. Somewhere close by, a horse whinnied and scuffed the sand.

A young child, a girl in rags, looked up at Petronia and Julius, her brown eyes pools of fear. She was sucking her thumb. With her other hand she grabbed on to Petronia's robe and clung to it tightly.

But Petronia barely noticed her, so horrified was she by the sight of the water that lay beyond them. Though the air was thick with dust, she could see that the sea was heaving strangely — not in waves, but like a gigantic cauldron of boiling scum, flecked with rocks and ash.

"You must take me! It's our only chance!" screeched a female voice.

Petronia recognized the voice of Flavia Theodora. The dishevelled woman stood by the pier that stretched out from the beach. A large boat was tied to the wharf, its elegantly curved bow bared as it tossed on the water. The churning sea banged the hull against the wooden planks of the pier.

Flavia was screaming at a young fisherman who was standing on the beach with a pair of oars in his hands.

"You're crazy!" he said harshly, shaking his head and pointing to the water. "Can't you see there is no escape here? The boat will be swamped in a minute out there."

"I have money! I can pay you," Flavia pleaded, showing him a handful of coins. "And my jewels, you can have them, too." Desperately she tugged at her two rings, but she couldn't get them off her fingers. She tore off her pearl earrings and pulled her two gold snakes' head bracelets from her arm, putting them into a small purse with the coins. Then she held the bag out to the fisherman. "Here, take it. My husband is a very wealthy man. There will be more to come, if you take me in the boat."

The man and the rest of the crowd simply

Trying to escape the mountain's fury, Petronia, with the baby Julius, and the soldier hurry down to the beach.

Overleaf: The last hours of Herculaneum.

stared at her, all at once quiet. It was as if they suddenly realized that if Flavia had no chance to escape, neither did they.

A wild look came into her eyes.

"Lizards and cowards, all of you!" she shrieked. "I'll do it myself!" And with that she grabbed the oars from the fisherman's hands and stumbled onto the pier. As the ash-flecked waves lapped at her feet, she fumbled with the ropes that bound the boat to its moorings. When the final knot came undone, she tossed the oars into the vessel and hiked up her robes to climb in.

At that moment, the earth shuddered beneath them, and the water seemed to rise up like a wall. In one quick second it crashed against the pier, tossing spongey-looking rocks onto the beach. In the next instant the water ebbed away, and the boat was gone.

Clutching a mooring post, Flavia stared at the water in disbelief. Her robes were drenched, her curls lank and filthy, plastered against her forehead. Still clutching her purse, she turned and swept past Petronia and the soldier. Like statues, the hushed crowd watched her go.

"I warned you, didn't I, you fools!" cried a hoarse voice above them. Looking up, Petronia saw a familiar figure balancing on the balustrade of the seawall that overlooked the beach.

"THE GODS ARE PUNISHING US!" 43

It was the crazy woman, Portia, weaving drunkenly, her hair standing out like Medusa's, as though full of snakes.

"The gods are punishing us, can't you see that?" she shrieked. "Did you really think there was any escape?"

Suddenly a fierce rumble shook the ground. Petronia felt it before she heard it. The seawall and the buildings above it seemed to lurch before her eyes. Then a huge cracking sound came from the direction of the town. Unable to tear her eyes away, the girl watched in horror as the balustrade tore away from the wall and Portia was hurled through the air down onto the beach. She crashed, face first, a short distance away, while an enormous chunk of stone hit the soldier in the back of the neck, knocking him flat.

The young boy in the boat chamber would have carried a house key similar to this one.

The force of the blast threw Petronia back onto the stone steps. She twisted away, pressing her shoulder against the wall that lined the steps, her head and arms shielding Julius while bits of rubble rained around them. When she finally looked up, a blast of heat and dust hit her in the face, so it was through a curtain of ash and tears that she saw the two dark mounds lying on the beach a stone's throw away.

Ignoring Julius's fresh sobs, Petronia scrambled to her feet and stumbled over to the bodies.

The soldier lay sprawled on his stomach, his sword trapped beneath him. Petronia knew he was dead, though she couldn't see his face, and there was no blood. Beside him, Portia lay in a crumpled heap.

The slave girl stood rooted, the horror finally sinking in. This was it, the end of the world. Portia had been right. Somehow, the gods had become so angry that they had sent the most terrible punishment possible. The jaws of the mountain would soon swallow them all.

Petronia felt a tug on her tunic. It was the little girl, her thumb out of her mouth now, her eyes pleading. In a daze, Petronia let herself be pulled away from the soldier, past the steps and the pier and along the beach. Where was everyone going? From inside one of the boat chambers lining the shore, she could hear the snort of a horse, and the sounds of people whimpering and praying to the gods.

The girl pulled Petronia toward one of the chambers. The air was thick with ash now, bitter and choking. Large pieces of rock began to fall — one grazed the side of her head and she stumbled, but it felt curiously light. Like one of the mistress's badly aimed blows, she thought absently.

She let herself be pulled into the boat chamber. Several people were already there, crouched together against the far wall, seeking shelter from the hail of rubble. But this group was quiet, not wailing. An oil lamp cast a pale glow over the cave.

A young boy huddling in a corner choked and gasped. Then his eyes closed, and he went silent. His fingers loosened, and something fell from his hand onto the dirt floor.

Petronia stared at the metal object. It was a house key.

She felt very calm now. It was becoming difficult to breathe. The rotten-egg stench was in her throat, her nose, her eyes, everywhere. But at least rocks were no longer falling all around her. Her knees collapsed beneath her and she closed her eyes. Such a waste, she thought suddenly, remembering the preparations for the banquet. All that food sitting there, and no one to eat it…

The last thing she realized was that the baby in her arms was still, and he was no longer crying.

Right: In a frenzy, the people on the beach run for shelter from the volcano's terrible blast.

CHAPTER SEVEN

The People on the Beach

Herculaneum, June, 1982

It was quiet on Herculaneum's ancient beach. Above my head, drying sheets and underwear fluttered from the apartment balconies that now overlook the ruins.

Today this beach is just a narrow dirt corridor that lies several feet below sea level. But thousands of years ago, the waves of the Mediterranean would have lapped where I now stood, and my ears would have been filled with the gentle sound of the surf, rather than the dull roar of Ercolano's midday traffic.

To one side of me stood the arched entryways of the boat chambers, most of them still plugged by volcanic rock, their secrets locked inside. Only one chamber had been opened so far, and its contents were now hidden behind a padlocked plywood door.

I eyed the wooden door longingly, wishing for a sudden gift of X-ray vision. Dr. Maggi, the keeper of the key, had been called away to a meeting with some government officials, and would not be back until sometime in the afternoon.

"*Dottoressa!*"

Ciro was calling me from farther down the old beach. He was waving me toward a roped-off area surrounding three ordinary-looking piles of dirt.

I have examined thousands of skeletons in my life, but seeing each one for the first time still fills me with a kind of awe. As I walked over to the mound that Ciro was pointing at, I knew I was about to meet my first Herculanean.

It didn't look like much at first — just a heap of dirt with bits of bone poking out. I knelt down and gently scraped earth off the skeleton, exposing it to the light for the first time in two thousand years. Although the skeleton was badly broken, I had a hunch that it might be female, but I was puzzled by the position of her bones. Her thigh was poking out grotesquely beside a section of skull. It almost looked as if the bones had been carelessly tossed there, they were so broken and tangled.

Then I realized that something dreadful had happened to this woman, and that she had met with a violent death of some kind. Her skull was shattered, her pelvis crushed, and her leg had been thrust up to her neck. Roof tiles were trapped beneath her.

I looked up. Above me was the open terrace where Herculaneans had held sacred ceremonies. Above that was the wall of the town itself, most of the surrounding balustrade now missing.

Had this woman fallen from the wall above? Had some huge force propelled her from the town, perhaps a piece of flying debris, or the blast from the volcano itself, so that she smashed face down onto the ground? What had she been doing on the wall in the first place? Calling down to the people on the beach for help?

I picked up one of the bones and felt its cool smoothness in my hands. Because this was the first Herculanean I got to know, this skeleton was extra special to me. I named her Portia.

By measuring the bones, I could tell that Portia was about 5 feet 1 inch (155 centimetres) tall. She was about forty-eight when she died — an old woman by Roman standards — and had buck teeth.

Above: The beachfront, the ruins of Herculaneum and Vesuvius as they look today.

Left: I closely examine each bone of a skeleton as I lift it from the wet volcanic earth.

Later, after a chemical analysis, we learned that Portia also had very high levels of lead in her bones. Lead is a poison, but in Roman times it was a common substance. It was used in makeup, medicines, paint pigment, pottery glazes, and to line drinking cups and plates. Cheap wine was sweetened with a syrup that had been boiled down in lead pots, so heavy drinkers may have had even more exposure to lead.

On either side of Portia was a skeleton. One was another female. She lay on her side, almost looking as if she had died in her sleep. As I brushed dirt from her left hand, something shiny caught my eye as it glinted in the sunlight. It was a gold ring.

When we uncovered the rest of the hand, we found a second ring. And in a clump on her hip we found two intricate snakes' head bracelets made of pure gold, a pair of earrings that may have held pearls, and some coins (the cloth purse that had probably once held these valuables had long since rotted away).

We ended up calling her the Ring Lady. She was about forty-five when she died. She was not terribly good-looking; her jaw was large and protruding. There were no cavities in her teeth, but she did have gum disease, which left tiny pits in the bone along her gum line. If she had lived today, her dentist probably would have advised her to floss more often!

In fact, most of the Herculaneans I examined had very good teeth, with only about three cavities each. Today, many of us have about sixteen cavities each, in spite of all our fluoride treatments, regular dental checkups and constant nagging to floss and brush! But the Romans had no sugar in their diet. They used honey, but not much, because it was expensive. Instead, the Herculaneans ate a well-balanced diet, including much seafood, which is rich in fluoride. Not only that, but they had strong jaws from

Top: I carefully place each bone in a plastic vegetable crate to be transported to my laboratory.

Above: The Herculaneans had good strong teeth because they ate no sugar. Here, I clean these ancient teeth much as you clean yours today...but without toothpaste!

chewing and tearing food without using knives and forks. And they did clean their teeth, scrubbing them with the stringy end of a stick rather than using a brush and toothpaste.

On the other side of Portia we dug up the skeleton we called the Soldier. He was found lying face down, his hands outstretched, his sword still in his belt. We found carpenter's tools with him, which had perhaps been slung over his back. (Roman soldiers often worked on building projects when they were between wars.) He also had a money belt containing three gold coins. He was quite tall for a Roman, about 5 feet 8 inches (173 centimetres).

When I examined the man's skull, I could see that he was missing six teeth, including three at the front, and that he'd had a huge nose. And when I exa-mined the bone of his left thigh, I could see a lump where a wound had penetrated the bone and caused a blood clot that eventually had hardened. Near the knee, where the muscle would have been attached, the bone was enlarged slightly. This indicated that he would have had well-developed thighs, possibly

Right: We called this skeleton the Ring Lady because of the two gold rings she wears on her left hand. We also found two bracelets, a pair of earrings and some coins by her side.

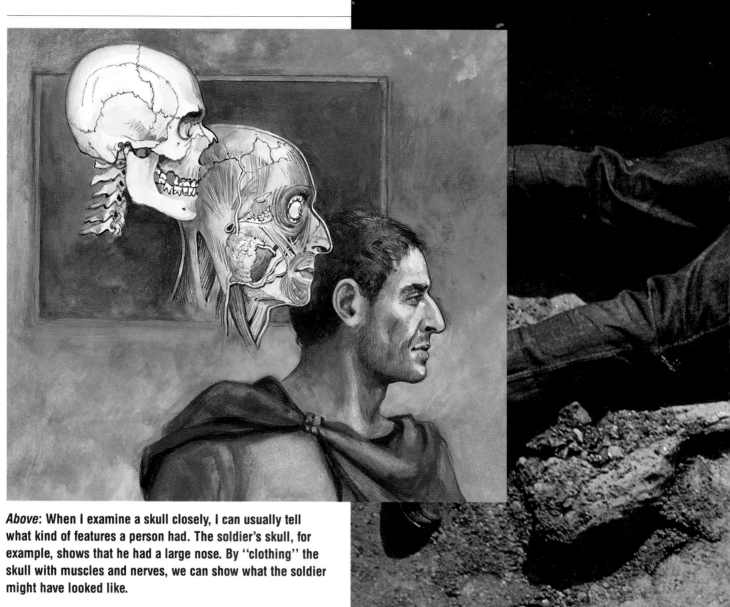

Above: When I examine a skull closely, I can usually tell what kind of features a person had. The soldier's skull, for example, shows that he had a large nose. By "clothing" the skull with muscles and nerves, we can show what the soldier might have looked like.

Right: An archaeologist carefully brushes dirt away from the soldier's skeleton. The soldier's sword still lies by his side.

due to gripping the sides of a horse with the knees while riding (Romans didn't use saddles).

Had the soldier lost those front teeth in a fight, I wondered. Had he been wounded in the leg during the same fight or another one? His life must have been fairly rough and tumble.

While members of the excavation team poured buckets of water on the three skeletons to loosen the debris, I continued to scrape off the dirt and volcanic matter with a trowel. Later, in the laboratory, each bone and tooth would be washed with a soft brush. Then they would be left to dry before being dipped in an acrylic solution to preserve them. Finally, each bone would be measured, then

measured again to prevent errors, and the figures would be carefully recorded.

By late afternoon my back and knees were stiff from crouching, and the back of my neck was tight with the beginning of a sunburn.

I stood up and stretched. There was still much to do before the three skeletons would be free of their volcanic straitjackets. I started to think about heading back to the hotel for a shower and bite to eat. But a flurry of activity down the beach caught my eye, and suddenly I no longer felt tired.

To my right, Dr. Maggi stood outside the locked wooden door I had seen earlier. He was unbolting the padlock. When he saw me, he

waved. I put down my trowel, wiped my hands on my jeans and hurried over. Inside, I knew, was the only group of Roman skeletons that had ever been found — the twelve people who had huddled in the shelter and died together when the volcanic avalanches poured down the mountainside into the sea.

I could hear an odd echo from inside the chamber as Dr. Maggi clicked the padlock

We found these coins in the soldier's money belt. One of them has the head of the Emperor Nero on it.

open. Behind me, a number of the crew members had gathered. We were all very quiet.

The plywood door seemed flimsy as Dr. Maggi pulled it open. From inside the chamber came the dank smell of damp earth.

A shiver crept up my neck. We were opening a 2,000-year-old grave. What would we find?

As I entered the cave-like boat chamber,

I could barely see, even though the sun flooded through the door. Someone handed me a flashlight, but its light cast greenish shadows, making it feel even more spooky.

The light played over the back of the shelter, no bigger than a single garage and still crusted over with volcanic rock. I saw an oddly shaped, lumpy mound halfway back. I took several steps into the chamber and pointed the light at the mound.

The narrow beam found a skull, the pale face a grimace of death. As my eyes grew accustomed

I took another step into the cave. At my feet was a skeleton that was almost entirely uncovered. From the pelvis I could see it was a female, a girl, lying face down. Beneath her, we could just see the top of another small skull.

It was a baby.

I knelt down and gently touched the tiny skull. My throat felt tight as I thought about this girl, this baby, and what it must have been like for them in this dark cave in the moments before they died.

"*Una madre col suo bambino,*" whispered Ciro behind me.

"I don't think they're a mother and baby," I said. I could see from the pelvis that the girl was not old enough to have had children. I pointed to my own stomach and outlined a beachball tummy with my arms while I shook my head. "This girl has never given birth."

"*Allora, è la sorella?*"

I frowned, pulled my Italian-English dictionary out of the back pocket of my jeans and flipped through it. I realized Ciro thought these two skeletons belonged to a baby and its older sister.

"We'll see," I mur-

Excavators have nearly cleared one of these boat chambers, but the one next to it is still blocked by hard volcanic rock.

to the dim light, I soon realized there were bones and skulls everywhere. They were all tangled together — clinging to each other for comfort in their final moments — and it was hard to distinguish one from another. But I knew that twelve skeletons had been found in all — three men, four women and five children. One child had an iron house key near him. Did he think he would be going back home?

mured. I knew it was important not to jump to conclusions. You have to question everything about bones, especially ones that have been lying around for two thousand years. I've known cases where people thought bone damage was caused by joint disease, when it was in fact caused by rats gnawing at the dead body.

I struggled to free a bronze cupid pin and two little bells from the baby's bones. Whoever the

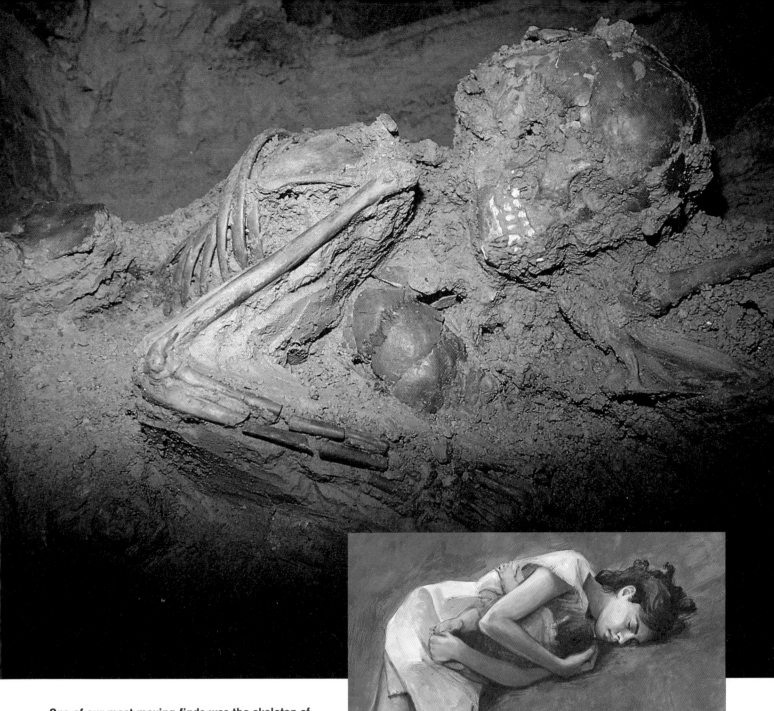

One of our most moving finds was the skeleton of a young slave girl cradling the tiny skull of a baby *(above)*. With these two skeletons, the tragedy of that terrible day in A.D. 79 became very real to us.

child was, it had been rich enough to wear expensive ornaments. But I knew it would take many more hours of careful study before we knew the real story behind these two skeletons.

Later, in the laboratory, I gained enough information to put together a more likely background for the skeleton of the young girl.

Unlike the baby, she had not come from a wealthy family. She had been about fourteen, and from the shape of her skull I knew she had probably been pretty. When I examined her teeth I could tell that she had been starved or quite ill for a time when she was a baby. She had also had two teeth removed about one or two weeks before she died, probably giving her a fair bit of pain. And her life had been very hard. She had done a lot of running up and down stairs or hills, as well as having to lift objects too heavy for her delicate frame.

Above: A coin box found on the beach.

Right: I clean the fragile bones of an ancient Roman.

Opposite page, bottom: Inside a boat chamber, a student pours water over tangled skeletons to loosen the debris.

Left: Among the ruins archaeologists found these unusual glass beads with tiny faces on them.

Right: An archaeologist carefully removes debris from the hull of a first-century Roman boat.

Bottom: Sometimes it can take as long as four days to glue a skull back together.

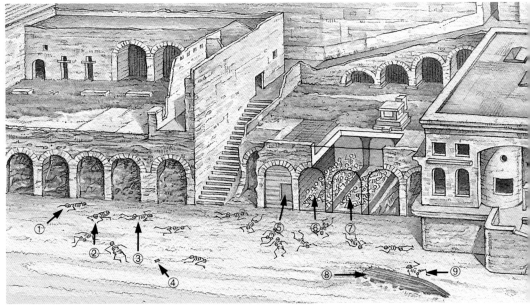

WHO WERE THE PEOPLE ON THE BEACH?

The illustration *(above)* shows how the ancient seawall looks today. Altogether, we excavated over one hundred skeletons from the beach and boat chambers.

1. The Ring Lady
2. Portia
3. The Soldier
4. Coin box
5. Chamber with 26 skeletons inside
6. Chamber with 40 skeletons inside, including one of a horse
7. Petronia's chamber, with 12 skeletons inside
8. The boat
9. A slave, perhaps a fisherman

This girl could not have been the child of a wealthy family, like the baby. She had probably been a slave who died trying to protect the baby of the family she worked for.

And there were many others. Near the slave girl lay the skeleton of a seven-year-old girl whose bones also showed that she had done work far too heavy for a child so young.

We found a sixteen-year-old fisherman, his upper body well developed from rowing boats, his teeth worn from holding cord while he repaired his fishing nets.

Particularly heartbreaking were the two pregnant women I examined, for we were also able to recover their tiny unborn babies, their bones as fragile as eggshells. One woman had been only about sixteen years old.

Though it is fascinating to reconstruct the life of a single person by examining his or her bones, for anthropologists and historians the most useful information comes from examining all of the skeletons of one population. This is one reason why Herculaneum is so important.

During the next few months we opened two more boat chambers. In one we discovered forty tangled human skeletons and one of a horse; in another we found twenty-six skeletons creepily lined up like a row of dominoes, as if heading in single file for the back of the chamber.

The skeletons represented a cross-section

WHAT BONES TELL US

The human skeleton contains about two hundred bones. Bones are rigid because they contain calcium — the same substance that is in eggshells and teeth. While you are alive, your bones are alive, too. Blood runs through them, they have their own nerves, and they grow and change shape and absorb chemicals, just like the rest of your body.

Once a body is dead, after the clothes and flesh have rotted away, the hard skeleton still holds many clues as to what the person was like when he or she was alive.

By "reading" and analyzing a skeleton, scientists can discover the person's sex, race and height. We can see approximately how old a person was at death, and

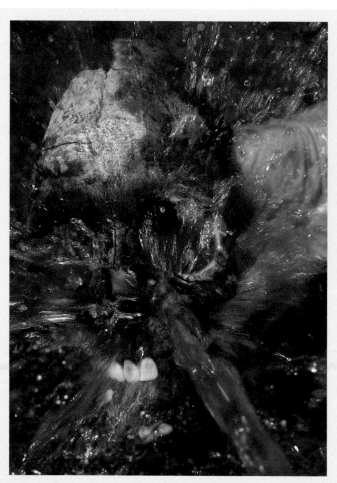
Hosing down an ancient skull.

approximately how many children a woman had. By looking at the way people's bones and teeth are formed, we can also tell whether they had certain diseases, or whether they had been starved or been sick as children. If we grind up a small piece of bone and put it in a chemical solution, we can analyze the solution in a laboratory and find out what minerals have been absorbed by the bone, which can tell us what kind of food a person ate.

Muscles are attached to bones. When muscles are used frequently, they become bigger and pull on the places where they are attached. The bones will then change shape to create more surface for the muscles to attach to. By examining the shape and weight of certain bones, we can see which muscles were used, and what kind of work or exercise a person might have done.

of the population of a whole town — old people, children and babies, slaves, rich and poor, men and women, the sick and the healthy. By examining all these skeletons, we can get some ideas about how the townspeople lived and what they were like physically.

We found out, for example, that the average Herculanean man was 5 feet 5 inches (165 centimetres) tall, the average woman about 5 feet 1 inch (155 centimetres). In general, they were well nourished. And we have examined enough people to know that although the rich people had easy lives, the slaves often worked so hard that they were in pain much of the time.

Studying these skeletons closely can also help medical researchers and doctors. In ancient times, many diseases could not be cured by surgery or drugs. Instead, people kept getting sicker, until they eventually died. By examining the bones of these people, we can learn a great deal about how certain diseases progress.

By the end of my stay in Herculaneum, I had examined 139 skeletons. Their bones were sorted into yellow

I spend day after day in my laboratory sorting, examining and gluing bones together.

The Romans usually cremated the dead and placed their ashes in urns like this one.

plastic vegetable crates that lined the shelves in my laboratory. And each box of bones has a different story to tell.

Even though I can't tell the good guys from the bad, and I can't tell you whether they were happy or not, I know a great deal about these people. I can see each person plainly. I even imagine them dressed as they might have been, lounging on their terraces or in the baths if they were wealthy, toiling in a mine or in a galley if they were the most unfortunate slaves.

Most of all, I feel that these people have become my friends, and that I have been very lucky to have had a part in bringing their stories to the rest of the world.

Epilogue

When I first came to Herculaneum in 1982, I expected to stay for five days. Those days have turned into years, but I wouldn't have missed them for anything.

After those heady weeks of digging out and examining the first skeletons, came many more of carefully cleaning, sorting, analyzing data and compiling endless notes. It has been lonely work much of the time. For ten months a year I have mostly worked by myself in my laboratory at the edge of the excavation site, each evening walking the two miles (three kilometres) back to my hotel room. I've missed my family, my home, my friends.

So far, less than half of the ancient town has been uncovered. The magnificent *palaestra* has only been partially exposed, and archaeologists know that there are probably dozens of other important buildings and treasures still buried. Less than half of the boat chambers have been opened so far. How many people lie in the others?

Should the rest of Herculaneum be dug up, even though this will mean demolishing the modern buildings lying on top of the site and

A portrait of a woman with a writing tablet from Pompeii.

putting many people out of their homes?

What should happen to the skeletons and artifacts when they are found? Should they be left where they are, so that visitors can see and be moved by the sight of the Herculaneans in their final moments — cradling their babies or clutching their valuables? If they are left alone, how will we keep them from disintegrating, or stop vandals and thieves from getting at them? What can be done about the buildings themselves, now exposed to the elements, their wall paintings fading in the wind and rain, the 2,000-year-old wood rotting away, the floor mosaics cracking and crumbling with each tourist that walks over them?

Or should the treasures and skeletons be removed from the site so they can be studied by scientists and perhaps placed in a museum? And how much will it mean to the visitors at these museums when they see a soldier's skeleton or a shapely wine jug sitting alone in a glass case? Will they be able to imagine the soldier's final moments, or picture the life of the slave girl who had to carry the heavy jug without spilling the wine, and who would have been beaten severely if the jug had been dropped and broken?

Why are we saving these things, and who are we saving them for?

And, of course, we can't forget Vesuvius herself. From my laboratory window I can look out and see the most famous volcano in the world, her slopes now green and peaceful. On some days she still spouts smoke and steam, and yet thousands of people live within a few miles of her peak. Since that August afternoon in A.D. 79, she has erupted over seventy times, on average once every twenty-seven years. The last eruption was in 1944, almost fifty years ago. When will the next one be?

There is now a sophisticated observatory located right on the mountain, which has been built to detect future eruptions. This observatory, equipped with the most up-to-date equipment, has made me, like the many others who live on the lower slopes, feel safe during the years I have lived and worked here. But what could we really do to save Herculaneum itself, if Vesuvius erupted again?

Will the buildings and treasures that have been so painstakingly dug out and cleaned be swamped again by glowing avalanches of ash and rock?

volcanic ash and mud that killed so many. In fact, this rich soil is the reason so many people live in this region. It is responsible for the famous vineyards and is so full of nutrients that four vegetable crops can be harvested each year.

But even while the volcano bubbles and smokes, we continue to work and live in her shadow. We spend years digging up and brushing off the towns and the people that she buried so many years ago. We carry on with our lives, just as those ancient Herculaneans did, because in our hearts we know that there's little else we can do.

The stories that the skeletons tell me bring the past to life once again.

It is very possible, even likely, that this will one day happen.

The slopes of Vesuvius are once again lush and growing, made especially fertile by the

No matter how advanced our civilization, how sophisticated our scientific equipment, how grand our art and our architecture, the forces of Nature, once unleashed, are greater than us all.

Glossary

acrylic solution: A liquid plastic which dries to form a hard clear coating.

A.D.: The abbreviation for *Anno Domini,* which refers to the new era beginning with the birth of Jesus Christ.

alabaster: The white form of a mineral called gypsum, which light can shine through.

anthropology: The scientific study of the human organism and human customs. A person who studies anthropology is called an *anthropologist.*

archaeology: The scientific study of people from the past and their cultures. An *archaeologist* is a person who studies archaeology.

artisan: A person who is skilled at making something, usually with his or her hands.

atrium: The central room in a Roman house.

balustrade: A row of supports topped by a rail, which ornaments a terrace or balcony.

bow: The front end of a boat.

calcium: Actually calcium carbonate, a compound found in bones, teeth, shells and eggshells.

candelabrum: A branched candlestick or lamp holder.

catalogue: A complete list of a number of objects in which each one is described.

ceramic: Refers to an object made by heating clay; pottery.

cicadas: A family of insects with transparent wings that can make shrill noises.

cremate: To burn a dead body.

cupid pin: A pin showing a naked winged boy, often holding a bow and arrow. Cupid was the Roman god of love.

disintegrate: To break down into pieces or a powder.

dormice: Small rodents, similar to mice or squirrels.

dottoressa: The Italian title for a woman who is a doctor or scholar.

excavate: To uncover an object, a skeleton or even an entire town by digging.

gem-cutter: A person who cuts and polishes precious stones.

Hercules: A hero in Greek and Roman myth, famous for his strength, who performed twelve great tasks.

hull: The frame or body of a boat without its masts, sails or rigging.

Isis: The Egyptian mother goddess who promised an afterlife to believers.

Juno: The Roman goddess of light, birth, women and marriage. She was called Hera by the Greeks.

Jupiter: The king of the gods. The Greeks called him Zeus.

magma: Molten rock material that moves within the earth. (Molten rock is rock made liquid by heat.)

Medusa: A woman in Greek myth who had snakes for hair and whose looks could turn people to stone.

mosaic: A picture or pattern made by setting together small pieces of stone or glass.

ochre: A mineral of clay and iron used as a paint or dye.

palaestra: A Roman gymnasium.

pantomime: An ancient Roman dramatic performance with few or no spoken words, but with a solo dancer and a chorus that tells a story in song.

pelvis: The large basin-shaped hip structure of a skeleton.

portico: A porch with a roof supported by columns.

pumice: Light volcanic rock with many small holes in it, like a hard sponge.

relief: A picture carved into a stone surface.

scabbard: A sheath or case for a sword or dagger.

solarium: A room enclosed with glass to let in the sun's rays. A sun room.

soothsayer: A person who predicts future events.

sulphur: A yellow, non-metallic element that smells like rotten eggs. Sulphur fumes often accompany volcanic activity.

stern: The rear end of a boat.

stucco: Plaster or cement used to cover or decorate a wall.

terracotta: Unglazed reddish-brown pottery.

theater (also spelled theatre): A building with a stage and seats in rising tiers which is used for dramatic performances.

wet nurse: A woman who breastfeeds another woman's baby.

THE BURIED TOWN THROUGH THE AGES

A.D. 79

● Mount Vesuvius erupts violently. Some of the people of Herculaneum try to escape by sea, but they suffocate in boat chambers by the beach. The town is buried under 65 feet (20 metres) of ash and pumice.

A.D. 203-1139

● Vesuvius erupts violently at least eleven times in this period. In the following centuries the volcano will erupt once every twenty-seven years on average, causing more ash and pumice to fall on the buried town.

1503

● A mapmaker named Ambrogio Leone draws a map of the region of Campania, in Italy, and marks Herculaneum close to its actual site for the first time in centuries.

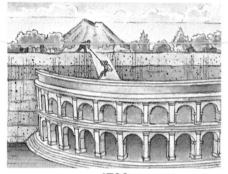

1709

● Workers digging a well in the town of Resina, built on top of Herculaneum, discover the ancient theater. An Austrian prince hears about the discovery and loots the theater of its beautiful marble and bronze statues.

1750-1765

● Karl Weber, an architect, discovers and draws plans of the Villa of the Papyri from an underground tunnel. Workers recover bronze statues and papyrus scrolls.
● Herculaneum's tunnels are closed. People become more interested in Pompeii, which is easier to excavate.

1828-1927

● Over the years more and more of Herculaneum is excavated.
● In the twentieth century, archaeologists use new machines and techniques to uncover a large part of the buried town.

1944

● Vesuvius erupts as the Allied forces attack Italy.
● Nazi chief Hermann Goering takes famous bronze statues that were once buried in Herculaneum from the museum in Naples. They are returned after the war.

1982-1988

● Ditch-diggers discover the first skeletons on Herculaneum's ancient beach.
● Dr. Sara Bisel excavates and studies these skeletons and those found in nearby boat chambers, telling the world for the first time what the Herculaneans were really like.

1990

● Two masked robbers with revolvers steal over 250 valuable artifacts from a Herculaneum storeroom, including the Ring Lady's jewels. These treasures have not yet been found.

Recommended Further Reading

Ancient Rome: Cultural Atlas for Young People
by Mike Corbishley 1989
(Facts on File Inc. U.K., U.S. and Canada)
An atlas of the Roman world.

City
by David Macaulay 1974
(Houghton Mifflin Company, U.S. and Canada/William Collins, U.K.)
An illustrated story of Roman planning and construction.

Earth: The Ever-Changing Planet
by Donald M. Silver 1989
(Random House Ltd., U.S.)
Includes volcanoes, earthquakes, glaciers, fossils and other fascinating aspects of earth science.

The Lost Wreck of the Isis
by Robert D. Ballard 1990
(Scholastic Inc. U.S./Random House of Canada Ltd./Hodder & Stoughton Publishers U.K./Ashton Scholastic, Australia)
The gripping story of the JASON Project's exploration of the deepest ancient shipwreck ever found.

Pompeii
by Peter Connolly 1990
(Oxford University Press U.K., U.S. and Canada)
A comprehensive look at the fascinating ancient city of Pompeii.

Tiberius Claudius Maximus: The Cavalryman
by Peter Connolly 1989
(Oxford University Press U.K., U.S. and Canada)
This book recounts the exciting life of a Roman soldier who lived in the first century A.D.

Volcanoes and Earthquakes
by Mary Elting 1990
(Simon & Schuster, U.S.)
All about two of nature's most awesome phenomena.

Some museums where you can see art and artifacts from ancient Rome:
The Archaeological Museum,
    Naples, Italy
Boston Museum of Fine Art,
    Boston, MA, U.S.A.
The British Museum, London, England
The J. Paul Getty Museum,
    Malibu, CA, U.S.A.
The Louvre, Paris, France
Metropolitan Museum of Art,
    New York, NY, U.S.A.
The Royal Ontario Museum,
    Toronto, Ont., Canada
State Art Collections, Dresden,
    Democratic Republic of Germany
State Hermitage Museum,
    Leningrad, USSR

Picture Credits

Front Cover: (Top) Painting by Ken Marschall (Left) © Jonathan Blair/Woodfin Camp and Associates (Middle) C M Dixon (Right) O. Louis Mazzatenta © National Geographic Society
Front Flap: Pedicini
Back Cover: (Top) Painting by Laurie McGaw (Bottom) © Jonathan Blair/Woodfin Camp and Associates
Back Flap: Joe McNally © 1984 Discover Publications
Poster: (Top left) Painting by Laurie McGaw (Bottom left) C M Dixon (Middle) Painting by Ken Marschall (Right top) Diagram by Jack McMaster (Bottom left) Painting by Laurie McGaw (Bottom right) Cheryl Nuss © National Geographic Society
Endpapers: C M Dixon
Mosaic Border: Margo Stahl
Page 1: Scala/Art Resource, NY
2-3: Painting by Pierre-Jacques Volaire, Giraudon/Art Resource, NY (Inset) Scala/Art Resource, NY
6-7: Painting by Ken Marschall
8-9: © Jonathan Blair/Woodfin Camp and Associates (Top inset) C M Dixon (Bottom inset) O. Louis Mazzatenta © National Geographic Society
10: © Jonathan Blair/Woodfin Camp and Associates
11: (Top) Archaeological Exploration of Sardis (Bottom) Courtesy of the Royal Ontario Museum, Toronto, Canada
12-13: Painting by Laurie McGaw
14: C M Dixon
15: Metropolitan Museum of Art, Rogers Fund, 1903.
16: C M Dixon
17: (Top left and right) Scala/Art Resource, NY (Bottom) Diagram by Jack McMaster
18: C M Dixon
18-19: Painting by Laurie McGaw

20: Scala/Art Resource, NY
21: (Left, top right) Scala/Art Resource, NY (Bottom right) Borromeo/Art Resource, NY
22: Courtesy of the Royal Ontario Museum, Toronto, Canada
23: Painting by Laurie McGaw
24: (Left) Scala/Art Resource, NY (Right) C M Dixon
25: (Top left and right) Scala/Art Resource, NY (Bottom left) C M Dixon
26: O. Louis Mazzatenta © National Geographic Society
27: Painting by Laurie McGaw
28: Joe McNally © 1984 Discover Publications
29: Painting by Pierre-Henri de Valencienne, courtesy of the Musée des Augustins, Toulouse, France
30: (Top and middle) Map and diagram by Jack McMaster/Margo Stahl
31: © Steven Muir/EARTH IMAGES
32: (Top) Diagram by Jack McMaster/Margo Stahl (Bottom) Pedicini
33: (Middle) Werner Forman Archive (Bottom left) Ancient Art & Architecture Collection (Bottom right) C M Dixon
34: Courtesy of John Penniston
35: (Left) Diagram by Jack McMaster/Margo Stahl (Right) Ancient Art & Architecture Collection
36: Alinari/Art Resource, NY
37: (Top) Art Resource, NY (Left) Werner Forman Archive
38: (Middle) The J. Paul Getty Museum, Jack Russo (Bottom) Scala/Art Resource, NY
39: Jonathan Blair © National Geographic Society (Inset) Diagram by Jack McMaster/Margo Stahl
40: Courtesy of Sara Bisel
41: O. Louis Mazzatenta © National Geographic Society (Inset) Art Resource, NY
43: Painting by Laurie McGaw
44-45: Painting by Ken Marschall
46: Courtesy of the Royal Ontario Museum, Toronto, Canada
47: Painting by Laurie McGaw

49: (Top) O. Louis Mazzatenta © National Geographic Society (Bottom) Jonathan Blair © National Geographic Society
50: Cheryl Nuss © National Geographic Society
51: O. Louis Mazzatenta © National Geographic Society
52: Painting by Laurie McGaw
52-53: © Jonathan Blair/Woodfin Camp and Associates
53: O. Louis Mazzatenta © National Geographic Society
54: O. Louis Mazzatenta © National Geographic Society
55: (Top) O. Louis Mazzatenta © National Geographic Society (Inset) Painting by Laurie McGaw
56: (Top left) © Jonathan Blair/Woodfin Camp and Associates (Top right) Cheryl Nuss © National Geographic Society (Bottom) O. Louis Mazzatenta © National Geographic Society
57: (Left and bottom right) O. Louis Mazzatenta © National Geographic Society (Top right) © Jonathan Blair/Woodfin Camp and Associates (Middle) Diagram by Jack McMaster
58: Cheryl Nuss © National Geographic Society
59: (Top) Cheryl Nuss © National Geographic Society (Bottom) Courtesy of the Royal Ontario Museum, Toronto, Canada
60: C M Dixon
61: O. Louis Mazzatenta © National Geographic Society
63: Diagrams by Jack McMaster

Madison Press Books would like to thank the following people for their assistance and advice: Osvaldo Croci, O. Louis Mazzatenta and Carol L. Dumont of the National Geographic Society, Joyce and John Penniston, J. Richard Steffy of the Nautical Archaeology Program, Texas A & M University, and Steve Carey of the Graduate School of Oceanography, University of Rhode Island.